courageous
joy

More books by (in)courage

Take Heart: 100 Devotions to Seeing God When Life's Not Okay

For more resources, visit incourage.me.

AN
(in)courage
BIBLE STUDY

courageous joy

DELIGHT IN GOD
THROUGH EVERY SEASON

Written by Mary Carver
and the (in)courage Community

Revell

a division of Baker Publishing Group
Grand Rapids, Michigan

Published by Revell
a division of Baker Publishing Group
PO Box 6287, Grand Rapids, MI 49516–6287
www.revellbooks.com

Printed in the United States of America

Library of Congress Cataloging-in-Publication Data
Names: (in)courage (Organisation) I Carver, Mary (Writer), editor.
Title: Courageous joy : delight in God through every season / (in)courage ; edited by Mary Carver.
Description: Grand Rapids : Revell, a division of Baker Publishing Group, 2021.
Identifiers: LCCN 2020042201 I ISBN 9780800738099 (paperback)
Subjects: LCSH: Christian women—Religious life—Textbooks. I Joy—Biblical teaching—Textbooks. I Joy—Religious aspects—Christianity—Textbooks.
Classification: LCC BV4527 .C68 2021 I DDC 248.8/43—dc23
LC record available at https://lccn.loc.gov/2020042201

(in)courage is represented by Alive Literary Agency, www.aliveliterary.com.

21 22 23 24 25 26 27   7 6 5 4 3 2 1

contents

introduction

C hoose joy!"

It's a phrase we see everywhere, from embroidered pillows to hand-lettered graphics on Pinterest. It's a sentiment we give and receive in all sorts of circles, implying that a smile is the only acceptable expression a face can have and happiness is the only appropriate emotion a person should express. It's a biblical command that can, at times, feel confusing and callous as we try to figure out how exactly to choose joy and only joy.

But what if choosing joy isn't as straightforward as we've been led to believe? What if it's less about the look on our face and more about the state of our heart?

"Rejoice in the Lord always. I will say it again: Rejoice!" (Phil. 4:4 CSB).

It's a command. It's an invitation. It's a Bible verse and, for some of us, a song lyric we can't help humming each time we see the words.

But what if this encouragement to rejoice is not just one more item on our "be a good Christian" checklist but rather is a gift from God? What if this emphasis on joy—echoed on T-shirts and tattoos and stickers that adorn our water bottles and laptops—is *for* our good instead of a way for us to *be* good?

The joy of the Lord is so much deeper, so much more life-giving than the joy of this world. It's longer lasting than fleeting happiness and more contagious than the giggles of a child. (Although little-kid giggles might be one thing that brings us both worldly *and* holy joy!) Joy in the Lord is more than a catchphrase or a consolation prize when life gets hard. And though it's impossible to find joy on our own, we are never actually left alone in our quest for it. God freely offers both the courage to seek joy and every reason to find it. He *is* our joy, and He shares our joy.

Courageous joy is both breathtakingly simple and beautifully complex. And it's what we're going to investigate over the next six weeks.

You won't find a dictionary definition of "joy" in the Bible. Rather, you'll find repeated invitations to rejoice and to shout for joy, as well as dozens of ways to do just that. From God's incredible creation and the hope we find in knowing Him, to forgiveness, friendship, and even facing trials, the list of reasons to find joy in the Lord is long and runs from Genesis through Revelation.

Sometimes, though, we struggle to find joy—even when we know and love the Lord. And sometimes joy shows up in a tangle of other emotions, and we're unsure which thread to pull. Joy is often found in the company of gratitude and hope; surprisingly, it's also available through grief and weariness. For most of us, if we had to describe our relationship with joy, we would say, "It's complicated."

This Bible study about courageously seeking and sharing joy will help. Together, we will dive into the Word of God to learn what He says about joy. We'll learn to find joy in every circumstance we face and to share it with everyone we encounter. We'll begin to understand how a person can truly count it *all* joy, even when the "all" we're given is not the "all" we were hoping for or expecting. Together, we will make Psalm 100 our anthem:

> Make a joyful noise to the LORD, all the earth!
> Serve the LORD with gladness!
> Come into his presence with singing!
> Know that the LORD, he is God!
> It is he who made us, and we are his;
> we are his people, and the sheep of his pasture.

> Enter his gates with thanksgiving,
>   and his courts with praise!
>   Give thanks to him; bless his name!
> For the LORD is good;
>   his steadfast love endures forever,
>   and his faithfulness to all generations. (ESV)

How to Use This Study

Courageous Joy is a great study for personal or small group use. If you're doing it with a group, we recommend allowing at least forty-five minutes for discussion, or more for larger groups. (We think groups of four to ten people work great!) Enhance your community study experience with our *Courageous Joy* leader guide and videos. To download your free small group resources go to www.incourage.me/leaderguides.

Each day of this study has a lot to take in. As you work through it, don't feel like you have to complete it all in one sitting. Just like God doesn't want choosing joy to be another thing we check off our list in order to earn a prize, we don't intend for this study to be something that weighs you down with expectations. Will you be challenged? We hope so! But as you grow in faith and joy in the Lord, our prayer is that you will finish encouraged.

So work through this study at your own pace. Ask God to reveal His insight and truth to you. Then listen as He speaks to you through His Word.

Each week focuses on a different aspect of joy:

- **Week 1** begins with the foundational question, What is joy?
- **Week 2** reveals how we can find joy in God simply for who He is.
- **Week 3** explores the ways we can find joy in the way God made us.
- **Week 4** dives into our many expressions of joy in all the blessings God gives us.
- **Week 5** examines the obstacles to finding joy when life is hard.
- **Week 6** challenges us to find joy in and share joy with our communities.

Each week has a cadence that will help you get the most out of this study:

- **Day 1** looks at our call to courageously explore that week's topic.
- **Day 2** spotlights how Jesus or another key biblical figure lived it out and what we can learn from that person.
- **Day 3** tackles what the world says about that week's topic.
- **Day 4** shows us God's heart for you in that topic.
- **Day 5** closes the week with motivation for becoming a courageous woman.

We at (in)courage are excited to begin this *Courageous Joy* journey with you. You'll see that each day opens with a story from one of our writers sharing her experience of seeking joy. We hope these stories will help you feel less alone and more seen as you look for God in your own story.

Are you ready? Join us as we turn away from the world's counterfeit version of temporary satisfaction and embrace the deep, authentic joy God is offering.

what is joy?

Every good and perfect gift is from above, coming
down from the Father of lights, who does not change
like shifting shadows.

James 1:17 CSB

One day an ad from one of my favorite stores showed up in my email inbox. Splashed across the top in big letters was the phrase "JOY MAKERS." Of course, the ad was pointing shoppers to deals on toys, electronics, appliances, and cozy styles. Our Generation dolls, child-size John Deere electric tractors, smart TVs, Fujifilm Polaroid-style cameras, fleece jammies, and blanket scarves— apparently this is the stuff joy is made of.

The message was loud and clear: joy comes from having *stuff.* The pictures looked promising, but we all know better. Honestly, I love giving and receiving gifts. It's one of my top love languages. I love finding just the right gift for that wow factor or to make someone feel deeply loved.

That Christmas I paid attention during all the gift-getting and unwrapping. As my daughters, nieces, and nephews tore through piles of presents, there was excitement. There was laughter and merriment, but it only lasted for a time. Even though I love gifts, I've realized through the years that no gift brings true lasting joy.

Our culture too often confuses joy with happiness. Joy is more nuanced than happiness. Joy emanates out of God's unconditional and fierce love for us, while happiness can be fickle and fleeting, like a quickly forgotten Christmas present. In other words, joy is a state of being rather than an emotion.

For example, you might feel happy on Christmas morning when you unwrap the gift you really, *really* wanted but never expected to get. But true joy moves beyond surface happiness. True joy comes in recognizing that the gift you received was provided through resources given by Yahweh Yireh, our Provider.

Jesus models for us how to have joy in all circumstances. The deep joy that He experienced with His Father enabled Him to endure death on a cross. Joy is not just choosing to think happy thoughts. It's choosing to clothe ourselves with an *attitude of joy* only accessed through the Holy Spirit.

—DORINA LAZO GILMORE-YOUNG

Where do you most often find yourself looking for joy?

We're told that every good and perfect gift comes from God (James 1:17) and to give thanks to God for everything (Eph. 5:20). And we know that joy and gratitude are closely linked. After researching these topics for twelve years, psychologist Brené Brown said she didn't find a single person who described themselves as joyful who didn't actively practice gratitude. Contrary to her presumptions going into the research, her actual findings were that "practicing gratitude invites joy into our lives."[1]

So then, if we are grateful for a birthday present or a new job, a commute without red lights or a notice that the new book we've been waiting for is available at the library, or any number of gifts we might receive on earth, does that mean we are finding our joy in earthly things?

Should we ignore those things and only focus on spiritual matters? How should we define "good and perfect gift" or "spiritual matters"? The letters of Paul can help us work through these questions as we grow in our faith and joy.

Read Colossians 3. Notice the repetition of the words "earth" or "earthly" and "whatever you do." Record what stands out to you.

_____

_____

_____

_____

_____

_____

_____

Paul wrote this letter to the church at Colossae to remind them of the basics of the Christian faith (chapters 1–2) and to provide instructions for daily living (chapters 3–4). In chapter 3 he urges us to "set your minds on things above, not on earthly things" (v. 2) and "put to death what belongs to your earthly nature: sexual immorality, impurity, lust, evil desire, and greed, which is idolatry" (v. 5 CSB).

He also uses the phrase "whatever you do" twice in this chapter:

> And whatever you do, in word or in deed, do everything in the name of the LORD Jesus, giving thanks to God the Father through him. (v. 17)
>
> Whatever you do, do it from the heart, as something done for the LORD and not for people. (v. 23)

Though Paul was writing a letter to one particular church, he understood that his words would reach many others as well. Therefore, he knew he could not possibly give detailed instructions for every situation that a believer might encounter. Instead, he presents readers with both specific examples and general guidelines to help us live out our faith according to God's will—no matter what situations we are in or what we are doing. One of those guidelines is to be thankful and express gratitude.

What does this understanding of Colossians 3 tell you about the things you should be grateful for? What are some gifts you've received that come from God?

What are some ways you can live out your faith in "whatever you do"? As you reflect on different areas of your life, do you see any that could use redirection toward God?

Paul's letter to the Philippians gives further insight and examples of how we should focus our minds. He has a lot to say about courageous joy, and we'll dive into Philippians 4:4–7 later in this study. But today let's focus on the sentence directly following that passage about joy:

> Finally brothers and sisters, whatever is true, whatever is honorable, whatever is just, whatever is pure, whatever is lovely, whatever is commendable—if there is any moral excellence and if there is anything praiseworthy—dwell on these things. (Phil. 4:8 CSB)

Different translations of the Bible express that final command in different ways. The Christian Standard Bible quoted above uses the phrase "dwell on these things," while several other versions translate it as "think about these things." The New Living Translation says to "fix your thoughts on [these things]," and *The Message* paraphrases it as "you'll do best by filling your minds [with these things]."

Want to experience real, lasting joy? Add to your list of thanks anything that is true, honorable, just, pure, lovely, commendable, or excellent. Forgiveness for a cutting remark. An encouraging word from a friend. An answered prayer. Victory over a recurring sin. Provision from that new job. Think about these things! Dwelling on the goodness of God and all that He gives us directly impacts how we experience the joy of His love.

> **Dwelling on the goodness of God and all that He gives us directly impacts how we experience the joy of His love.**

Read Philippians 4:8 in several translations (use a Bible app or visit BibleGateway.com). Write down what things you will fix your mind on, what you'll dwell on or think about this week.

_____

_____

_____

_____

_____

_____

Digging deeper for the true source of our joy sometimes leads to a realization that our mind needs realignment. As you courageously examine your mindset this week, call out the things you're dwelling on that don't fit into the Philippians 4:8 parameters. How is your joy renewed when you turn your focus to God's good gifts?

_____

_____

Reflect on this prayer and make it your own today:

Heavenly Father, thank You for the many gifts You give me. Even if I never receive another thing, Lord, I'm so thankful for my salvation in Jesus! I know that I can get sidetracked sometimes, focusing on things that don't matter nearly as much as what You have for me on earth and in heaven. Please realign my heart with Yours and help me set my mind on You. Amen.

For the LORD your God is living among you.
    He is a mighty savior.
He will take delight in you with gladness.
    With his love, he will calm all your fears.
    He will rejoice over you with joyful songs.

Zephaniah 3:17

My almost-two-year-old niece shrieked at me from across the room. "Liza!" Her grin was so wide it showed the gap between her teeth. I love that gap. "Liza! Liza!"

"Selah!" I cried with the same enthusiasm, although it was hard to match hers. "How are you, my girl?"

A group from our church was meeting in a small Presbyterian church basement to pray over our community. Selah launched her toddler body into my legs, and I scooped her up, leaving a trail of kisses along her cheeks and head. A friend from my church laughed when she saw Selah's excitement.

"She's so happy to see you," my friend said. "Kind of reminds me of God."

"What do you mean?" I asked. Selah squirmed in my arms. I put her down and she ran off to play with her older brother.

My friend came closer. "I just think that must be how God feels about you—He must always be so happy to see you."

I had never thought of it like that before. But whenever I see Selah, and whenever Selah sees me, we both can't help but burst into huge grins, immediately touching and kissing and hugging. If I am that happy to spend time with my niece, how much happier would God be to spend time with me?

"Think about it," my friend said. "We never picture God happy. But I think He's probably the happiest person in the world."

I looked over at Selah playing. I watched her for a minute. Joy bloomed in my heart at the thought of God being even more happy and excited to spend time with me than I am with Selah. It was nothing God said and nothing God did, but just who He is. A joyful God who beams and bursts with excitement at the thought of spending time with me.

—ALIZA LATTA

Who are you most excited to see after a long (or short) absence? How do you feel when you see or hear from that person? Can you imagine God feeling that way about you?

As Jesus traveled to Jerusalem for the last time before His arrest and crucifixion, He interacted with a lot of people—teaching, healing, and in some cases even angering them. After hearing the Pharisees and scribes complain again about His habit of spending time with sinners, Jesus turned to the crowd that had gathered. To a group of religious leaders and teachers, sinners, and tax collectors (who were commonly known as traitors and thieves and widely despised in those days), He told three parables.

A parable is a simple story that teaches a spiritual lesson. Jesus often used this form of teaching, and Luke 15 records three of His parables.

Read Luke 15. What three things are lost in the stories Jesus tells? What was their significance to their owners? To what lengths did the owners go to find their lost items?

_____

_____

_____

_____

Have you ever lost something of great value? What did you do to find it? If you did find it, how did you react? Recount that story here.

_____

_____

_____

_____

It's interesting to note that Jesus didn't only share these stories with what *The Message* calls "men and women of doubtful reputation." Jesus knew that the religious leaders—the same ones He sharply criticized for not practicing what they preached (Matt. 23)—were also listening. And He spoke accordingly, sharing a message that both obvious sinners and so-called saints needed to hear.

In describing the great joy of the shepherd, the woman, and the father, Jesus explained why He spent so much time in the company of sinners. As He's recorded saying in the Gospel of Mark, a doctor is needed by the sick, not the healthy (2:17). In the same way, these parables illustrate just how much God values those who are far from Him and how determined He is to reach them. Jesus knew His mission was to reach the lost, and He wasn't going to be distracted by what religious leaders—those who professed to already know God—thought was appropriate.

After the parables of the lost sheep and the lost coin, the third story Jesus tells is more complex. The story of the prodigal son is clearly a metaphor about the joy God feels when we return to Him, despite our great sin. However, the story doesn't just end with the father and his younger son reunited; it also tells us about the father's older son—the one who stayed, who did what was right, and who was clearly resentful of the warm welcome his brother received.

The lost are important to God, and He will go to the greatest lengths to find them and welcome them back.

Through these parables Jesus told the crowd that the lost—those who are far from God—are important to God. He will go to the greatest lengths to find them and welcome them back. And when something (or someone) lost is found, it's time to rejoice.

Which of these three parables speaks most meaningfully to you? Which person (or lost item) can you most easily imagine yourself as? Which one is harder to relate to or understand?

Imagine the angels throwing a huge heavenly party on your behalf, rejoicing because you have found your way back to God. Picture Jesus crying out, "She was lost, but now she's found!" He told us that's exactly what happens every time one sinner turns back to God and follows Him. The way we feel when we find our lost keys or wallet, when we uncover a lost treasure in our attic, or when we run into an old friend at the store pales in comparison to the way God rejoices when His children return to Him. Like the shepherd, the woman, and the father in Jesus's parables, God is saying, "Rejoice with me!" He's inviting us into His joy. Will you join Him?

Take another look at Luke 15:10. Write it out here, but replace the phrase "one sinner" with your own name. Spend some time considering what this verse means with regard to God's love for you. How does this change your view of God or of yourself?

_____

_____

_____

_____

_____

_____

_____

_____

If you've never turned from sin and found your way back to God, today is the day to do that. If you are a follower of Jesus but have gotten off course, today is the day to come back home to the Father. Write your heart in a simple prayer. Turn to Him, ask His forgiveness, and let His love wash over you as you rejoice together.

_____

_____

_____

_____

_____

_____

Reflect on this prayer and make it your own today:

Thank You, Jesus, for spending time with sinners and saints. You know which one I've been, and You know who I am today. And I know that any distance between us is too much. I want to come home, God. I want to return to Your arms, Your shelter, Your path and plan for my life. Please forgive me. Thank You for looking for the lost and celebrating when You find me. I love You. Amen.

May the God of hope fill you with all joy and peace as you trust in him, so that you may overflow with hope by the power of the Holy Spirit.

Romans 15:13 NIV

A few years ago when my high school class was planning a reunion, a former classmate mentioned in a side conversation how my Facebook posts are always positive. It was strange the way he said this like it was a bad thing. Apparently, staying positive and choosing joy isn't cool. It's way cooler and supposedly more sophisticated to put on a facade of apathy and cynicism—or at least that's what internet memes and late-night talk shows tell us.

I was surprised to hear this person's impression of my online posts, because authenticity matters to me and I'd believed the lie that the only way we can "be real" is by complaining or criticizing. After that conversation, however, when I went back and scrolled through my Facebook page, I saw that most of my posts were, indeed, pretty positive. And for the record, they were honest in the way I'd hoped as I shared real life through a lens of determined joy.

After more than a few years of letting bitterness and cynicism take root in my heart, those words I shared on social media were evidence I was finally learning to choose joy no matter my circumstances. And if that leads to a few people rolling their eyes or calling me a Pollyanna, I'm okay with that, because I hope it might also lead a few people to ask where I find the strength to choose joy on even the hardest days.

My hope is that someone will wonder why it matters so much to me to choose joy, look for reasons to celebrate, and count my blessings and gifts.

My hope is that one day I can tell my classmate or a neighbor or even a stranger on the internet exactly where I get my joy and why I am determined to spend my days chasing it down and holding on tightly. I can't wait for the next time I get to explain that my joy comes from the Lord.

—MARY CARVER

Has anyone ever questioned your authenticity or criticized you for expressing joy or looking for the silver lining in a situation? How did that make you feel?

_____

_____

_____

_____

We often think that sharing our darkest emotions, such as fear, anger, or doubt, makes us most vulnerable. But the opposite can be true. Expressing joy requires our heart to be open and therefore vulnerable as we share our pleasure or appreciation. Expressing our joy shows people what makes us tick, how we are wired, who we are. And that can be scary!

Opening ourselves up in that way takes courage we can only get from the Lord. Thankfully, we can be confident He will give us that strength not only because He promises to do so (Isa. 40:28–31) but because His Word commands us to rejoice. In a passage we will return to several times throughout this study, Paul writes to the church in Philippi, "Rejoice in the Lord always. I will say it again: Rejoice!" (Phil. 4:4 CSB).

Read Psalm 46. Write down the words used to describe the Lord. Some translations say the Lord is a "fortress," while others call Him a "stronghold." What do those words, along with other descriptors used in this psalm, tell you about God?

_____

_____

_____

_____

When you think about expressing joy to the world, do you feel scared or nervous? Does joy ever make you feel vulnerable? If God is your refuge and strength, how does that change your perspective on sharing joy?

_____

_____

_____

_____

As we consider that God will give us the courage we need to vulnerably feel and share joy, let's make sure how we think about joy aligns with God's Word instead of with the world's definition. What is joy, after all? Is it the same as happiness? Is it simply looking for the silver linings or being grateful for what you have? If you're still wrestling to put joy into understandable terms you can hang on to and live out, it may help to read how other brothers and sisters in the Lord have explained it.

John Piper says, "Christian joy is a good feeling in the soul, produced by the Holy Spirit, as He causes us to see the beauty of Christ in the word and in the world."[2] Henri Nouwen had quite a bit to say about joy, including this: "Joy is the experience of knowing that you are unconditionally loved."[3] He also said, "Joy is based on the spiritual knowledge that, while the world in which we live is shrouded in darkness, God has overcome the world."[4]

When writing about joy, Chrystal Evans Hurst says God is the "true, life-giving fountain of joy. When you believe in Jesus, you have something to look forward to every single day. You know that your sins are forgiven along with the beautiful fact that you have an opportunity to have a relationship with Him. It can't get any better than that."[5]

Which of these descriptions resonates most strongly with you? Take a moment now and write your own definition of joy. What is it? Where does it come from? What does it look like and feel like?

Mother Teresa also described joy, saying, "Joy is prayer. Joy is strength. Joy is love. Joy is a net by which we catch souls."[6] Though the metaphors are different, this perspective on joy seems similar to that of Paul in his letter to the Romans. In Romans 15 he writes that he wants the believers in Rome to have so much joy, peace, and hope that they overflow with it. And why else would we need to have an overflowing joy if not to "catch souls"?

Paul knew that finding joy in the Lord would help us to love one another better and that in loving one another we would also find joy. Romans 15:13 says, "May the God of hope fill you with all joy and peace as you trust in him, so that you may overflow with hope by the power of the Holy Spirit" (NIV). This verse comes just after Paul encourages us to follow Jesus's example in putting others' needs before our own and just before Paul discusses the importance of sharing the Good News with the world.

Our goal in seeking and finding and choosing and sharing joy is to be so compelling, so attractive to those who don't know God, that they ask why. Our hope in the Lord should be so great and give us such abundant joy that we are called to explain ourselves (1 Pet. 3:15). And in that moment, when our joy has become so alluring and contagious, we can be confident that God will give us the courage and clarity to share exactly where our joy comes from and where others can find it too.

> **Our goal in seeking and finding and choosing and sharing joy is to be so compelling, so attractive to those who don't know God, that they ask why.**

Read Romans 15. How does the context of Paul's message about loving one another and sharing the gospel affect your understanding of verse 13? Write verse 13 in your own words here.

_____

_____

_____

_____

_____

How can you courageously open yourself to joy today? How can you then share that joy with another person?

_____

_____

_____

_____

_____

Reflect on this prayer and make it your own today:

Dear Lord, thank You for loving me so much that You would give Your life and pay for my sins! Thank You for Your promises, for being my refuge and strength. You give me so much hope and joy I can barely contain it. Please give me courage to open my heart to receive all the joy You have for me—and to share it with the world. Thank You, Jesus. I love You. Amen.

Therefore, since we are surrounded by such a huge crowd of witnesses to the life of faith, let us strip off every weight that slows us down, especially the sin that so easily trips us up. And let us run with endurance the race God has set before us. We do this by keeping our eyes on Jesus, the champion who initiates and perfects our faith. Because of the joy awaiting him, he endured the cross, disregarding its shame. Now he is seated in the place of honor beside God's throne.

Hebrews 12:1–2

I am able to love in ways that are not my preference. To do taxes even though numbers aren't my jam. To scrub toilets when I think there are more holy items on my to-do list. To cuddle my child when I need alone time. To prepare a meal even when I'm tired. But why do I love this way?

Jesus said, "If anyone would come after me, let him deny himself and take up his cross and follow me" (Matt. 16:24 ESV).

God is teaching me that carrying my cross sometimes looks like loving people in the way that they need, rather than loving them the way that I want to or the way that's most convenient. I carry my cross in everyday ways, private ways, mundane ways, loving others through those sacrifices. And then God's love pours out of me.

What if we follow Jesus and carry our cross like we are told to? That thing we are avoiding because we don't enjoy it, or because it feels like it's beneath us, or because we figure we aren't cut out for it—that could be the very thing necessary to truly love God and our neighbor.

Our friends will notice when we die to our own needs in order to help them. Our spouse will feel loved when we finally do that one thing he would really appreciate without complaining. Our children will remember how we spent focused time with them even though other things may have been calling our name.

I carry my cross and die a little more to myself.

I carry my cross and complain a little less.

I carry my cross and grow closer to the Father because that's the only path to Him.

I carry my cross and see the joy set before me.

I carry my cross and can forgive those who didn't invite me.

I carry my cross and my family feels loved.

Jesus endured the cross for the joy set before Him (Heb. 12:2). The joy set before Jesus was *us*! The full measure of Jesus's joy is His desire for those who belong to Him. Those we love will feel a small portion of that joy when we carry our cross every day in obedience and focus our gaze on God.

—STEPHANIE BRYANT

Do you find joy in serving others with love? If that's a difficult practice for you, why do you think that is?

_____

_____

_____

_____

_____

As we discussed yesterday, Paul knew that serving others in love would bring us great joy and that the joy we receive from the Lord would empower us to love others better.

In the New Living Translation, Romans 15:1–2 reads, "We must not just please ourselves. We should help others do what is right and build them up in the Lord." Paul quickly moves on to explain the reason behind this instruction: "For even Christ didn't live to please himself" (v. 3). He reminds us that "Christ came as a servant to the Jews" (v. 8).

Not content to simply tell his readers that they should serve one another, Paul then asks God to help them do what doesn't come naturally: "May God, who gives this patience and encouragement, help you live in complete harmony with each other, as is fitting for followers of Christ Jesus" (v. 5).

Read Romans 15 again. Perhaps read it in a different translation than you did on day 3. (You can easily find different translations by using a Bible app or at BibleGateway.com.) Reflect on Paul's reasoning for why believers should serve others even to the point of sacrificing themselves. Do you think this kind of service could bring you joy? Do you think it could be a way of sharing your joy?

Read Romans 12:10 and write it here in your own words. How do you think this relates to chapter 15? What do you think Romans 12:10 would look like in your life?

_____

_____

_____

_____

_____

_____

In the book of Hebrews we read about the role joy played in the crucifixion of Jesus: "Because of the joy awaiting him, [Jesus] endured the cross, disregarding its shame. Now he is seated in the place of honor beside God's throne" (Heb. 12:2). The original language here could also be translated "instead of the joy," implying that Jesus traded the joy of heaven's glory to come to earth as a man, live a life without sin, and endure a painful death to take the punishment for all of humanity's sin.[7] Because He loved us so much (John 3:16), He laid aside His heavenly glory and privileges as God and instead received the punishment we deserve (Rom. 6:23). All of that is consistent with everything we know from Scripture about God and His Son, Jesus.

Some interpreters look at this statement from another angle, examining what joy Jesus could have found that would be great enough for Him to endure the cross. Though our human minds cannot easily comprehend being selfless enough to die for another (especially when Jesus could have stayed in paradise with His heavenly Father), for Jesus it was worth it because of what came after His sacrifice. When you look at the cross from Jesus's perspective, it makes sense that He would have been willing to give up His seat in heaven for a time to live and die on earth *and* be overjoyed with how God used His sacrifice.

Read Hebrews 12:2. Write here what joy you think awaited Jesus after He endured the cross. Now read it again and replace "because of the joy" with "instead of the joy." How does that change your understanding of Jesus and the joy of His sacrifice?

_____

_____

_____

_____

_____

As you reflect on Jesus's joy, both in heaven and on earth, how does that affect your own feelings of joy? How does it affect your approach to serving others in love, metaphorically carrying your cross for others like Jesus carried His cross for us?

_____

_____

_____

_____

_____

Jesus found joy in His great love for us, and He put that love into action with the ultimate sacrifice. In His victory over sin and death, He suffered for every one of our sins in obedience to God the Father's magnificent plan, then rose again on the third day and destroyed the

May we discover fresh joy by extravagantly and humbly serving one another in love.

power Satan had over humanity. In today's opening story, Stephanie shared how she finds joy in serving others and growing closer to the Lord. Let's be women of courage who follow Jesus by carrying our cross too. May we discover fresh joy by extravagantly and humbly serving one another in love.

How can you lean on God's strength and follow Jesus's example to love and serve others this week?

_____

_____

_____

_____

Reflect on this prayer and make it your own today:

Dear God, I'm sorry I haven't always been a humble, loving, or joyful servant. Please forgive me for only serving others to get something in return or for serving with a resentful heart. Thank You for the incredible example of Jesus, who saves me from my sin and shows me how to give up my own needs and comfort for others. I know doing that will bring me the joy You offer and give me the chance to share that joy. Please help me carry my cross today, Lord. Amen.

Be glad in the LORD and rejoice,
you righteous ones;
shout for joy,
all you upright in heart.

Psalm 32:11 CSB

I grew up as a pastor's kid in a denominational culture that prioritized lofty knowledge. I memorized and recited catechisms and Bible verses, I had theological debates, and I felt most secure in my faith when I was serious, when I knew more than the next person, when I could prove my point with theologically based evidence.

But deep down inside I was also a kid who loved to delight. I loved the way autumn leaves would flitter about as they fell with little care or precision. I relished the way movies could bring to life the impossible, fantastical narratives I read in books and imagined in my head. I found deep joy in gathering at the table to eat and being fed by one another's company and life.

Delight and faith didn't seem to coincide, however; they were of different worlds that seemed wrong to overlap. But as I matured in life and in faith, becoming more childlike as I grew, I paid more attention to the many feasts described in the Old Testament and I realized how serious God is about celebration. Each significant moment in the Israelites' history was marked with a festival and rituals to remember what God had done: Passover, Purim, and the Feast of the Tabernacles, just to name a few. This included eating, singing, shouting, reading Scripture, righting wrongs, forgiving debts, and welcoming others.

It's in celebrating that we remember God—His faithfulness, His goodness, His ever-present help. It's the practice and discipline of rejoicing that teaches us to pause, to align our perspective with God's, and to see that celebration and faith aren't meant to be separated. Instead, the two are deeply woven together so we can know God, not only in head knowledge but also from our lived-out experiences as His beloved children.

—GRACE P. CHO

Which was emphasized as more important in the religious tradition or the family you were raised in: knowledge or joy? How did that affect your faith?

For many of us, facts are so much safer than feelings. Memorizing lists and verses and numbers requires hard work and focus, but it doesn't necessarily engage our hearts. And opening our hearts to feelings like delight and joy can make us feel vulnerable.

When we share knowledge with someone, we are merely transmitting information. But sharing joy with someone? Like we talked about on day 1, that requires letting people see who we are. The things in which we find joy are like a window to our souls, revealing what matters most to us. And what matters more—and therefore leaves us most vulnerable when we talk about it—than our faith?

C. S. Lewis wrote, "To love at all is to be vulnerable. Love anything, and your heart will certainly be wrung and possibly be broken. If you want to make sure of keeping it intact, you must give your heart to no one."[8] Brené Brown says, "If you ask me what the most terrifying emotion we experience as humans is, I would say joy."[9] On the other hand, Scripture tells us, "Rejoice in the Lord always. I will say it again: Rejoice!" (Phil. 4:4 NIV). And just as the Lord encouraged Joshua when he faced his own terrifying situation, He encourages us today, "Have I not commanded you? Be strong and courageous. Do not be frightened, and do not be dismayed, for the LORD your God is with you wherever you go" (Josh. 1:9 ESV).

> **The things in which we find joy are like a window to our souls, revealing what matters most to us.**

Do you think opening yourself to joy—true delight in the Lord and His creation, His good plans, and His love for you—requires courage? Why or why not?

What do you think it would look like for you to be strong and courageous as you choose joy?

As Grace discovered, we don't want a faith that's only based on obtaining and sharing head knowledge. But we don't want to be controlled by our emotions either. Proverb 29:11 says, "A fool gives full vent to his spirit, but a wise man quietly holds it back" (ESV).

So we don't want to be overly emotional, but we also don't want to be cold or clinical. Which one is it? If we turn to Scripture, we find encouragement to seek both wisdom and joy. In fact, Peter writes about how affection (guided by our hearts) and discipline (guided by our minds) are connected and useful in our faith journey:

> In view of all this, make every effort to respond to God's promises. Supplement your faith with a generous provision of moral excellence, and moral excellence with knowledge, and knowledge with self-control, and self-control with patient endurance, and patient endurance with godliness, and godliness with brotherly affection, and brotherly affection with love for everyone.
> The more you grow like this, the more productive and useful you will be in your knowledge of our LORD Jesus Christ. (2 Pet. 1:5–8)

Nearing the end of his life, Peter wrote this letter to urge believers to resist false teaching by continuing to grow in both faith and knowledge. In other words, he encouraged them to worship God and live out their beliefs with both head and heart.

Read the following passages:

Matthew 22:37–38

Mark 12:30–31

Luke 10:27

Why do you think Jesus instructed His followers to love God with all their heart *and* all their mind?

_____

_____

_____

_____

_____

What does it look like for *you* to love God with all your heart? What does it look like for *you* to love Him with all your mind?

_____

_____

_____

_____

_____

Experiencing joy might open us up in a way that makes us feel vulnerable, but it's crucial to the development of our relationship with

God. And rather than being something separate from our knowledge and wisdom, it's closely related. We can find great joy in God's love (Ps. 90:14) and His presence in our lives (Ps. 16:11). And we can be confident that when our traditions or our tendencies or even our fears tempt us to hold back our delight in the Lord, He will give us the courage we need to rejoice.

Using the columns below, write what you know about God (knowledge) and what delights you about Him (joy). Reflect on this list as you pray today.

Knowledge	Joy

How might you bravely incorporate joy into your pursuit of God's wisdom this week? Who will you let into your heart by sharing the things about the Lord that bring you joy?

Reflect on this prayer and make it your own today:

Dear Lord, You are so complex! I'm so glad that You not only want me to know facts about You but that You long for me to find pure joy in knowing You. Please give me courage to open my heart as You flood me with Your joy. Please show me how to love You with all my heart, all my mind, and all my soul. Amen.

joy in the Lord

I have loved you even as the Father has loved me. Remain in my love. When you obey my commandments, you remain in my love, just as I obey my Father's commandments and remain in his love. I have told you these things so that you will be filled with my joy. Yes, your joy will overflow!

John 15:9–11

My high school English teacher always cried while reading literature aloud. One minute Mr. Allison's voice filled the classroom with the poetic words of Hemingway, Fitzgerald, or Thoreau as we followed along with the text at our desks. The next minute, silence. Slowly, thirty teenagers looked up to find Mr. Allison wiping away tears and trying to regain his composure.

As a sixteen-year-old, I didn't quite understand how our quirky and passionate teacher could be moved to the point of tears by stories in books written what seemed like forever ago. Now, a couple decades later, I understand a little bit better. Words carry weight. Stories tap into deep parts of our experiences, our imagination, our longings—parts that we may not easily access or express on a regular basis.

While I've read novels and memoirs that have triggered a salty trickling of tears, nothing has awakened a well of unexpected emotion like the Greatest Story ever written in words and lives—the gospel.

More than any romance novel, overcomer story, or poetic prose, the Word of God has stirred my heart and filled me with new hope and fresh joy. Sure, there have been plenty of times I've tripped over long biblical genealogies or old cultural customs I didn't quite understand. There are some tough teachings and commands that aren't always comfortable to digest. But the more I study the Bible, the more I learn to read it for the totality of what it is: a love story.

It's the story of God's crazy love for all His messed-up kids, of which I am definitely one. It's the story of how He uses ordinary, awkward, imperfect people to do great things for His kingdom. How He turns our broken pieces and dusty ashes into something beautiful. Most of all, it's the story of how God loves His people so much that He made the unfathomable choice to give His perfect Son in exchange for a restored relationship with us.

This story is the basis of our joy. Of who God is and who we are as His kids. I'll join the ranks in getting choked up about a story like that any day.

—BECKY KEIFE

Have you ever cried while reading, hearing, or watching a story? What stirs your emotions most often or easily?

_____

_____

_____

_____

_____

Hours before He was betrayed, beaten, crucified, and forsaken by His Father, Jesus gathered with His closest friends and followers to eat the Passover meal, what we call the Last Supper. There in the upper room, He prepared His disciples for the time when He'd no longer be with them physically and promised them increasing joy through it all. Though Jesus's words were spoken before His death, resurrection, and return to heaven, they beautifully illustrate the redemptive story of God's love for us.

Jesus's great love for us, His promise to continue loving us, and His provision for us when He had to leave—it's all there in Scripture, and it's enough to bring a person to tears. And Jesus knew it. He knew that when His friends realized that He loved them to the point of death and laid down His own life for them (John 3:16), they would be overwhelmed with love, gratitude, and incredible joy.

Imagine you were present at the Last Supper. If you somehow knew that it was the last time you would be with Jesus, what would you have wanted to hear? What reassurances or explanations or promises would have filled your heart with joy? Do you see those reflected anywhere in Scripture? (You can read John 14–17 for the specific things Jesus taught on this occasion.)

_____

_____

_____

_____

_____

_____

_____

Read the following passages and write down the adjectives that describe God's love for us. Then, in your own words, answer these questions: How much does God love you? How would you describe His love for you?

2 Chronicles 6:14

Psalm 36:7

Jeremiah 31:3

Romans 8:31–39

The story of God's love for us is a joy-filled tearjerker, for sure. But Jesus spoke of another source of His joy: *obedience.* "When you obey my commandments, you remain in my love, just as I obey my Father's commandments and remain in his love" (John 15:10). Was Jesus attaching strings and conditions to His love? Of course not. As we read in Romans 8:38–39, absolutely nothing can separate us from the love of God. Nothing!

Rather, Jesus was explaining to His disciples that obeying the Father is an integral part of His love for the Father. And that love, which brought Him such great joy, could be ours as well. Oswald Chambers explained it like this: "The joy of Jesus was the absolute self-surrender and self-sacrifice of Himself to His Father, the joy of doing that which the Father sent Him to do."[1]

Following God's commands doesn't mean heaping on a burden (1 John 5:3) or obeying out of fear. Obedience is our invitation to follow God and walk with Him—trusting that His ways and plans are best. Obeying God is one way we love Him and draw closer to Him. That's something to rejoice about and exactly what Jesus wants for us.

Read John 15:9–17. How does Jesus describe the connection between love, obedience, and joy? How might it require courage to live out what Jesus is asking? How will this life of love-fueled obedience lead to joy?

Trying to explain to the disciples why His message was so crucial, Jesus promised that these life-changing words would lead to joy—so much joy that it couldn't be contained. Again, listen to Jesus's words: "I have told you these things so that you will be filled with my joy. Yes, your joy will overflow!" (John 15:11).

God's great love for us meets us in the middle of our grief and hardships.

Does overflowing joy mean the absence of sorrow? No. God's great love for us meets us in the middle of our grief and hardships. His love and presence can bring us to the same place as Isaiah, who declared, "I am overwhelmed with joy in the LORD my God!" (Isa. 61:10).

What are you overwhelmed with today? Reread the words of Jesus in John 15:9–11 and reflect on God's great love for you.

Throughout Scripture, God frequently tells us to trust Him (Prov. 3:5–6), to allow Him to carry our burdens (Ps. 55:22), and to be strong in Him (Eph. 6:10)—all things that require some measure of courage. How do you think obeying these commands could bring you joy? If you're feeling discouraged, ask God to infuse you with fresh courage. Then decide how you will seek that joy this week.

Reflect on this prayer and make it your own today:

Heavenly Father, I can hardly comprehend Your great love for us. Thank You for loving us so much! I want to respond to Your love and obey You—to show You how much I love You, to grow closer to You, to receive all the blessings You have prepared for me. Please give me courage to follow You wherever You take me, and pour Your love and joy into my heart through the Holy Spirit. Thank You, God. Amen.

Jesus called the children to him and said, "Let the little children come to me, and do not hinder them, for the kingdom of God belongs to such as these. Truly I tell you, anyone who will not receive the kingdom of God like a little child will never enter it."

Luke 18:16–17 NIV

Every time I'm in a worship service and the song leader suggests we raise our hands in praise, I cringe. I get a little sweaty and my mind starts racing.

What is wrong with you? Why can't you raise your hands?

I know. I should raise my hands. I want to. I do. But . . .

What if I look weird? What if they notice?

It's just not like me. I'm not a raise-your-hands kind of girl.

You mean you're not a praise-the-Lord kind of girl?

Just. Raise. Your. Hands.

Ahhh! It's not a big deal, but it feels like a big deal!

Isn't it enough to tap my foot?

Is this song ever going to—oh good, it's over now.

Every time.

Growing up in a small-town, traditional hymn-singing church, it never even occurred to me to raise my hands during worship until I witnessed my friends doing just that in college. In fact, closing my eyes while belting out my favorite songs was as expressive as I got back then—*and even that felt out of place.*

One Sunday, though, my internal debate was interrupted by my five-year-old standing next to me. As soon as she saw me notice her raised hands, she wanted to talk about it. "Mommy, why aren't you holding your hands up? Look! I'm holding up my hands for Jesus! You do it too, Mommy!"

So for once, I did the thing that my heart often longs to do but that feels so awkward and even scary: *I raised my hands.*

The specific way we worship isn't the point. The point is that for years I've ignored the urge to let go and worship the way that expresses my true feelings. I've remained content to worship half-heartedly because what others might think was more important to me than what God has placed in my heart and what I long to say to Him.

For my daughter, though, it was so much simpler than that. She heard the worship leader suggest we raise our hands, she felt joy as she sang about Jesus, and she raised her hands up high to express all those things. *Just like that.*

Oh, to be courageously joyful like a child!

—MARY CARVER

Have you ever been afraid of what others might think about the way you worship? How does that affect your ability to connect with God?

People worship God in so many different ways. Expressing our love and gratitude and joy in the Lord shouldn't be about how we look or following a set of rules. And yet sometimes we can feel intimidated or embarrassed when it comes to worship.

But do you know who never seems to feel self-conscious or reluctant to share their true feelings? Children.

When children sing songs to and about the God they've been taught loves them, their unblemished, unabashed joy cannot be contained. Without filters or fear, they jump and sing and dance their praise to the Lord, never afraid of what the kid jumping and singing and dancing next to them might think. Why can't we do the same?

Jesus knew we could learn much from observing little children. In Luke 18:16–17, He urged His followers to be more like children (see also Matt. 18:2–4; 19:13–14; Mark 10:13–16).

Does expressing your feelings about God and to God make you feel nervous or self-conscious? What do you think it would look like for you to worship God like a child?

_____

_____

_____

_____

_____

Raising your hands, dancing, or singing at the top of your lungs is not necessarily more holy or joyful than other styles of worship. Perhaps you feel more connected to God when folding your hands, kneeling, or even spending time in nature. Worshiping God with courageous joy simply means responding to God in the way He created you to be in relationship with Him, rather than allowing your expressions of joy to be affected by fear, uncertainty, or perceived expectations.

Worshiping God with courageous joy simply means responding to God in the way He created you to be in relationship with Him.

An example of someone who was unafraid of what others might think is the woman who poured expensive perfume on Jesus's feet, washing them with her tears and wiping them with her hair. This woman, who was known as a sinner in her community, interrupted a dinner hosted by a religious leader and knelt at the Lord's feet to offer Him her thanks and praise.

> One of the Pharisees asked Jesus to have dinner with him, so Jesus went to his home and sat down to eat. When a certain immoral woman from that city heard he was eating there, she brought a beautiful alabaster jar filled with expensive perfume. Then she knelt behind him at his feet, weeping. Her tears fell on his feet, and she wiped them off with her hair. Then she kept kissing his feet and putting perfume on them. . . . And Jesus said to the woman, "Your faith has saved you; go in peace." (Luke 7:36–38, 50)

Jesus explained to the confused men at the dinner table that the woman's dramatic behavior reflected her tremendous gratitude and love. She had been forgiven much, so she loved much (7:47). His point—to the religious leaders then and to us now—is that we have all been forgiven much. So shouldn't our response to Him be just as great?

Read the following verses:
John 3:16
Romans 5:8
Ephesians 2:8–9
1 John 3:1

How do you feel when you think about how much God loves you and what He has done for you? Describe those feelings here. If it helps, write down a couple of specific ways you've experienced God's lavish love and things you've been forgiven for.

_____

_____

_____

_____

Though the relationship we have with God comes from our heart, Jesus also said that what comes out of our mouth is a reflection of what lives in our heart (Luke 6:45). How does (or doesn't) what you say reveal the joy in your heart?

_____

_____

_____

_____

Think of a child you know or perhaps imagine your younger self. Can you picture her dancing and twirling through the temple courts as described in Psalm 100, singing with delight—smile wide and eyes bright—at the sheer anticipation of being in God's presence? Watch in your mind's eye as the Father wraps His child in a huge embrace.

That is the wonder of God's love. *That* is the joy available to us today because we know our hope and salvation are secure in Jesus (John 10:28).

Psalm 66:1–2 says, "Shout for joy to God, all the earth; sing the glory of his name; give to him glorious praise!" (ESV). Describe what it would look like for you to live this out.

Sometimes being a woman of courage means embracing joy and worshiping with childlike abandon. How can you be brave and authentically share your joy this week?

Reflect on this prayer and make it your own today:

God, I love You so much! I do. When I think about how much You love me—enough to come to earth, live a sinless life, and die for my sins so we would no longer be separated—I want to shout it from the rooftops! I can't contain my joy—or at least I don't want to. But sometimes I don't know what to say, or I'm afraid of looking foolish in front of others. Will You give me the courage to share my joy with abandon—before You and before others? Thank You, God. Amen.

Lord, there is no one like you, and there is no God besides you, as all we have heard confirms.

1 Chronicles 17:20 CSB

A close friend and I were on a neighborhood walk one day when she delivered a verbal jolt. I had been lamenting how someone who "should have" been leading me in my faith was failing miserably. This person who was supposed to build me up was letting me down, or at least that's how it felt to me. I was fundamentally assigning blame (without meaning to) because of their position.

"Have you ever considered that God might be prying your fingers off idols you're clinging to in place of Him?" She went on to challenge me to consider all the ways I might be holding on to people or things at the expense of my relationship with Christ. I began contemplating how I was filling my voids. How was I numbing my pain? I was grasping for worldly things to bring relief, satisfaction, and happiness without realizing I had pushed God to the margins.

My conversation with my friend that day ushered in a season of self-examination, and I began to recognize subtle forms of personal idolatry. At times my job, family, hobbies, service, even church activities or pastors—*all good things!*—were taking the place reserved for God alone. An idol could be anything that occupied my time, whether in thought or deed. It could also be anything in which I was finding identity, value, pleasure, or truth. Even how I spent money was telling.

We all need people in our lives who love us enough to tell us what we need to hear, don't we? It may *feel* better to hear what we want, but that sure doesn't help us. I am so thankful to have friends who point me to Jesus at the risk of hurt feelings or an uncomfortable or awkward moment.

That conversation was a starting point for me to see how easily I was willing to substitute happiness derived from people or things for the lasting joy that comes from knowing God deeply and intimately.

This glorious, indescribable joy that comes from loving and trusting God is available now and forever. Why would any of us settle for second best?

—ROBIN DANCE

Have you ever realized you have stopped putting God first in your life? What are some good things you have prioritized over God's best? List them here.

_____

_____

_____

_____

The road to idolatry is a slippery slope, isn't it? Discerning between good and best can be so difficult—impossible, really, without God's wisdom. That's how many of us find ourselves inadvertently worshiping the things of this world, even good gifts from God, rather than God Himself. Robin's story shows how easy it can be to let God slip from having first priority in our heart and to allow the counsel or leadership of a person to become more vital in our everyday life than His wisdom and discipleship.

How many of us have placed a pastor, writer, or mentor on a pedestal reserved for the Lord? Or perhaps you've found your idols closer to home in your spouse, children, career, ministry, organizational skills, hospitality gifts, or accomplishments. These are not *bad things*. God has given us many gifts, and it is good to enjoy and appreciate them. It's when we stop there—reveling in or relying on God's gifts but forgetting to let them lead us right back to the Lord—that we get in trouble. So often we trade true, lasting joy in the Lord for the fleeting happiness of false idols.

Read Matthew 6:19–21. What did Jesus say would happen to our earthly treasures? Have you experienced something that was once a source of pleasure becoming a source of pain? Describe that experience here.

_____

_____

_____

_____

_____

A few verses later Jesus tells His followers not to focus on (or worry about) what they will eat or wear. Then He tells the disciples, "Seek first the kingdom of God and his righteousness, and all these things will be added to you" (Matt. 6:33 ESV). What does that tell you about the importance of putting God first?

_____

_____

_____

_____

_____

What good is an idol? No good at all, says the Lord. The earthly things we find temporary hope and happiness in, the things we let creep into the innermost parts of our heart, the things we prioritize over simply being in God's presence and worshiping Him—those things are worthless compared to the abundant life we're promised in Christ (John 10:10). We shouldn't trade what might seem so good in the moment for the absolute best God is offering us.

> **We shouldn't trade what might seem so good in the moment for the absolute best God is offering us.**

Read Psalm 18:1–6, 16–19, 46–50, where David details all that God has done for him and what he's thankful for. (The entire psalm is worth reading if you have the time!) Then write your own list of thanks for God's best in your life.

_____

_____

_____

_____

_____

When David prayed, "LORD, there is no one like you, and there is no God besides you" (1 Chron. 17:20), God had just prevented him from building a temple in Jerusalem. Though building a physical house for the Lord would certainly have been a good thing, God knew it could easily become an idol in David's life. And He knew David would receive so much more joy—the kind that lasts longer than even the strongest temple—when his devotion was not divided.

Perhaps you've experienced something similar—making the task of your daily quiet time more important than the actual time you spend in God's Word, placing more importance on a ministry you lead than the God who calls us to good deeds, or putting your family first instead of remembering the One who created them. When that happens, God sometimes chooses to give us a nudge—like the conversation Robin had with her friend—to remind us where to find true joy.

Though David grieved the loss of a building project, he knew God's goodness and faithfulness. Similarly, Robin knew that, even though people may fail her and other good things may try to distract her, only God is steadfast and trustworthy. In our own moments of redirection, may we find the courage and joy to say with David, "As for God, his way is perfect: The Lord's word is flawless; he shields all who take refuge in him. For who is God besides the Lord? And who is the Rock except our God? It is God who arms me with strength and keeps my way secure" (Ps. 18:30–32 NIV).

Take a look at your calendar, your bank statement, and your heart. Based on what you see, where are you looking for joy, significance, or security right now? Make a list of things—even the good things—that might have become idols in your life.

If you have found idols in your life, it's time to put them back in their place—and that's not always easy, especially when those idols happen to be people or relationships. How will you courageously adjust your priorities so that your joy is dependent on God alone?

Reflect on this prayer and make it your own today:

Dear God, please forgive me for the ways I unintentionally cling to people and things instead of to You. I don't want to keep trying to squeeze joy out of what was never intended to fulfill me. Train my heart and mind to reach for You first, Lord. I know true joy is found in Your loving presence. Give me the courage to unclench my fists from idols and open my hands to Your goodness. Thank You for loving me—as imperfect and in-process as I am. I love You too. Amen.

I will celebrate in the LORD;
I will rejoice in the God of my salvation!

Habakkuk 3:18 CSB

Nearing the end of college, I found myself between apartments with no good options for my next home. I made my community aware of my need and I prayed for provision. Soon afterward, the director of Fellowship of Christian Athletes, a campus ministry I was involved in, and his wife invited me to stay in their guest room. It was abundant provision. I was welcomed in every way into their family. We broke bread, made memories, and had adventures. We believed God for big things and grew in faith together.

Over and over I have seen God show up in the kindest of ways. He has tangibly shown me His extravagant love through His body, the church. He has provided for my every need. In these past two decades of walking with the Lord and His church, I can think back to countless times of lack and need that I couldn't possibly have met on my own. When I was laid off from work and when I experienced several natural disasters, the Lord faithfully spoke to friends who blessed me financially or with groceries. When I've walked through times of personal crisis, friends have showed up with prayers and encouragement in ways that made all the difference.

I've been a believer for twenty years, and I can honestly say that I love the Lord even more today than I did when I first believed. I have a history with God that fills me with such joy, a history that gives me hope when times get tough. The first love I felt for Him, though—when He swooped in and rescued me from my sin, shame, failure, hurt, pain, and grief—was amazing and has created a foundation for my relationship with the Lord. Since then, He has healed me from the inside out, saving me from a life without Him.

There is so much of the Lord that I don't know yet, but what He's revealed fills me with such love. What we know should be a delight to us, and what we don't yet know should be a wonder to search out. This I know: God is good.

—KARINA ALLEN

Have you ever thought about the difference between loving God for what He does and loving Him for who He is? What parts of God's character bring you the most joy?

_____

_____

_____

_____

Separating our gratitude for everything God has done from our admiration for who God is can be tricky. But if we only appreciate God's favorable actions and answers, we will find it hard to rejoice in Him when life is hard and when we don't understand what He's doing. That may be why the final verses of Habakkuk are so noteworthy. Read them again in the English Standard Version: "Yet I will rejoice in the LORD; I will take joy in the God of my salvation."

Though you might not have encountered it much before now, the short book of Habakkuk has much to offer in our study of courageous joy, specifically as we look at what it means to find joy in the Lord. The prophet who wrote it felt deep sorrow and confusion as he looked at the world. Habakkuk took all his grief and all his questions to the Lord, who graciously answered him. The three chapters we find tucked away in the Old Testament are a record of their conversation.

After God reminds Habakkuk that He is still God and that His children must face the consequences of their sin, the prophet asks God for mercy and reminds *Him* of all the ways He's shown mercy in the past. But even if nothing good happens, says Habakkuk, he will still rejoice in the Lord. Even if the pain never ends, he will still find joy in the God of his salvation. Habakkuk shows us how to courageously face the reality of a hard situation and ask God for help, and then how to lean on the Lord's strength to find joy in Him no matter what the outcome.

Feeling the pain of a hurting world, asking God honest questions, choosing to love and trust and rejoice in Him even if He doesn't answer your prayers in the way you desire—these are all hard things! Which do you find easiest to do? Which is the most difficult?

Read Habakkuk 3:17–19 and rewrite it in your own words. (For example, "Even if I don't get the job or my house catches on fire or my kids get sick, I will rejoice in the Lord! He is strong and loving, and I'm amazed by Him! I know He will be with me no matter what.")

Jesus understood how much help we would need to continue trusting and finding joy in the Lord in the midst of challenging situations. When He spoke with His disciples at the Last Supper, He taught them many things, including how to live a life of love, obedience, and joy (like we talked about earlier this week). He was preparing them for His death and for His later return to heaven, comforting them in their sadness at the thought of being separated from their friend and teacher. He told them about the "helper" He would send in His place—the Holy Spirit—and He promised to return. "You have sorrow now, but I will see you again; then you will rejoice, and no one can rob you of that joy" (John 16:22).

Later, when Paul wrote to the Romans, he said God's love has been poured into our hearts through the Holy Spirit (Rom. 5:5). And later, when he wrote to the churches in Galatia, he said the result of having the Holy Spirit ("the fruit") is love, joy, peace, patience, kindness, goodness, faithfulness, gentleness, and self-control (Gal. 5:22–23). It's like God gave us a transfusion of joy when He gave us the Holy Spirit.

Simply being with God—and God being with us—is something to rejoice about! And just as Jesus promised that no one can rob

> **Simply being with God— and God being with us—is something to rejoice about!**

us of our joy, we also know that God will never leave us (Matt. 28:20). And we're not alone; we have the Holy Spirit helping us with everything. We have so much to celebrate!

Read Psalm 16 and list the reasons the author finds joy in the Lord. Make special note of the final verse of this psalm.

What situation in your life is hardest right now? How can you lean on the Lord's strength to courageously choose joy no matter how that situation turns out?

Reflect on this prayer and make it your own today:

God, I love You so much! And I know that sometimes I tend to feel love and joy most when I see the blessings You've given me. But today I just want to sit here with You and, instead of talking about my problems, I want to talk about You. You are incredible, Lord, and I'm overwhelmed with joy when I take time to really think about that. Thank You for being here with me. I love You. Amen.

This is the day the LORD has made;
let's rejoice and be glad in it.

Psalm 118:24 CSB

My perspective on finding joy changed one summer day after spending the afternoon with the youngest member of our family. We were all at my grandma's house, and my toddler niece wanted to be in Grandma's garden. But it was hot outside. So, so hot.

The last thing I really wanted to do was get all sweaty walking around the garden. I wanted to visit with the adults inside where it was air-conditioned. I asked the persistent three-year-old if she was sure she wanted to go outside. She was sure. That was the only thing she wanted to do. Reluctantly, I joined her, trying to hide my less-than-cheery attitude.

But my demeanor began to shift as I watched my little companion enjoy the wonder of the garden. She carefully stepped along each path, wandering through the flowers. I couldn't help but smile. Even in the heat and humidity of summer, with her rosy cheeks and her sweaty hair stuck to her forehead, she was as happy as could be. She was truly delighted with everything she saw.

She spotted a frog tucked under a plant and giggled as she pointed to it. "Oh, that frog is soooo happy!" she said.

Just like that, she reminded me of the simple joys in life. Joy that sometimes looks like a frog.

It would have been so easy to let the heat of summer, the sweating, and thoughts of air-conditioned comfort steal the joy of those wonder-filled garden moments. But sometimes we need to put all that aside and just dwell on God's beauty, dwell in His joy. He has given us so much!

I want to hold on to that kind of uncomplicated joy.

And so I take my lesson from a toddler. I don't want anything to steal or diminish the joy in my life. I don't want to miss what is right in front of me; life goes by way too quickly. I will stop to smell the flowers. I will smile at the frogs. I will delight in the uncomplicated beauty of pure, simple joy.

—JENNIFER UECKERT

Have you ever found joy somewhere completely unexpected? Describe where you found it and how that made you feel.

_____

_____

_____

_____

_____

Sometimes joy is hiding in plain sight, isn't it? Right there in the messy parts of life, something beautiful and surprising appears that reflects who God is. What a welcome surprise!

As adults, we sometimes make things overly complicated and miss the joy that's right in front of us. We're focused on a task at work, so we miss the beautiful bird perched outside our window. We're fixated on preparing dinner and checking the next thing off our to-do list, so we miss the curious question or belly laugh of our child.

The Old Testament prophet Elijah once spent many days on the run from the angry Queen Jezebel. He traveled through the wilderness and ate only what the Lord provided. Finally, Elijah came to a mountain where he waited through a windstorm, an earthquake, and a fire for the presence of God to pass by. He expected to encounter God in the wind, the earthquake, or the fire, but instead He heard the Lord speak in a gentle whisper (1 Kings 19:9–18). Like Elijah, we too forget that God often speaks in a still small voice—or even through a frog peeking out from behind a plant on a sticky summer day.

Think about the different ways God has revealed Himself and His joy to you. Describe some of those experiences here.

_____

_____

_____

_____

In Ephesians 1:18–19 (NIV), Paul prays that the believers in Ephesus would see God clearly. As you read that passage, think about who has helped you find God—and experience joy from knowing God—throughout your life. List those people here.

_____

_____

_____

_____

In today's story, Jennifer had to get down in the dirt to discover the joy God had planted for her niece that day. After all, that's where frogs are found! Dolly Parton is credited with saying, "The way I see it, if you want the rainbow, you gotta put up with the rain."[2] It's true. The only time we see a rainbow is when it rains. Of course, sometimes rain itself is something to celebrate; ask any farmer. For most of us, though, we don't like getting caught in the rain or having our outdoor plans ruined by the rain. But a rainbow! Who doesn't love a rainbow?

The rare sight of a rainbow is an important reminder for believers, as it represents a promise from God. In the book of Genesis, Noah received this promise: "When I send clouds over the earth, and a rainbow appears in the sky, I will remember my promise to you and to all other living creatures. Never again will I let floodwaters destroy all life" (Gen. 9:14–15 CEV).

God had flooded the earth to wash it clean of sin, but He knew that sin wasn't defeated and that we still needed to be rescued from its curse. However, He promised not to flood the whole earth again. The next time He washed our world clean, it would be through the blood of Jesus, and it would last forever.

No wonder we get so excited at the sight of a rainbow!

Looking for the rainbow after a storm isn't the same as merely "looking for a silver lining" when times are tough. When we live courageously, we can stand in the face of a storm with confidence because we know that, with God's help, we will not be overwhelmed. We know that God has promised to never leave us, and He's promised to rescue us without destroying us.

> When we live with courage, we can stand in the face of a storm with confidence because we know that, with God's help, we will not be overwhelmed.

What storm are you facing right now? What promises of God can you cling to while the metaphorical winds blow?

Rainbows and frogs aren't the only things that bring us joy. Everything God has created and every gift from His hand is an opportunity to turn our focus back to the Creator, giving Him glory and rejoicing in who He is. As we finish this week, may we never settle for second best or be distracted by what we see as inconveniences. May we keep our eyes on the Lord and shout for joy at every little and big thing we see.

Stepping outside our comfort zone to find joy in the Lord can be hard, but God is calling us to be strong and courageous in every part of our lives (Eph. 6:10). Will you let Him lead you into joy today? What will that look like for you?

Reflect on this prayer and make it your own today:

God, You are so creative, so kind, and so generous. Thank You for all the big and small ways You bring me joy! Thank You for opening the eyes of my heart to the truth of Your love and doing whatever it takes to make sure I don't miss it. Please keep my eyes and ears open for every bit of joy You have for me, Lord. Thank You. I love You. Amen.

joy in who God made you to be

I am sure of this, that he who started a good work in you will carry it on to completion until the day of Christ Jesus.

Philippians 1:6 CSB

No matter how hard I try, I really cannot park my small SUV straight inside a parking space. It's too big and too curved for my eyes and brain and hands to make that happen. I've tried. I've failed. And I'm cool with that. When it comes to parking my car, I'm like Popeye. "*I yam what I yam.*"

Of course, an inability to park is not a spiritual issue (even in the church parking lot). But as I was laughing to myself over that rant on my (lack of) parking skills, I started thinking about how often I pull a Popeye when it comes to other parts of my life.

Nearly every week my pastor says that God loves us no matter where we are in life—but He loves us too much to leave us there. I'm so grateful for that reminder of unconditional love, because I'm well aware that behind my Sunday morning mask is a woman who's incredibly imperfect and desperately grateful that God loves her anyway.

But what about the part where He loves me too much to leave me there in my sin and struggle and pain? What about feeling conviction over what I've been attributing to "who I am" as I read the Word, listen to a sermon, or sing along in worship? Well, that's a lot harder to handle. After all, I yam what I yam! This is the way God made me—isn't it?

Or . . . I could let God love me out of the place He finds me in today. I could confess the sin I've explained away as personality quirks and remember who I really am. Because who I really am? That person is the one God created and knows intimately and loves beyond measure. Who I really am is a child of God—and He loves me too much to leave me "the way I yam."

—MARY CARVER

Have you ever wanted to ignore a nudge or a twinge of guilt you felt about a behavior or habit you'd rather chalk up to just being how you were made? How does that compare to what God's Word says about how you were created?

Personality theories are all the rage right now. You can barely scroll through Facebook or visit Pinterest without seeing a quiz that will identify your Myers-Briggs personality type or a graphic guessing which Enneagram number best describes the characters in your favorite TV show. Learning about our personalities—what makes us tick, where our motivations lie, what our tendencies are—is fun and can be helpful when we use the information to better relate to others and to allow God to show us strengths and possible areas for growth.

Whether you've been delighted or devastated (or maybe even both) to learn more about yourself, you know that one of the most satisfying parts of getting personality test results is the feeling of being seen. It can be so meaningful to read an explanation that makes you feel understood in a deeper way, or perhaps even for the first time. But despite the ability of any person or test to understand and describe who we are, only our Creator knows us in the most profound way possible. As the psalmist says:

> O LORD, you have examined my heart
>   and know everything about me.
> You know when I sit down or stand up.
>   You know my thoughts even when I'm far away.
> You see me when I travel
>   and when I rest at home.
>   You know everything I do.
> You know what I am going to say
>   even before I say it, LORD. (Ps. 139:1–4)

The God of all creation, our heavenly Father, created you and knows everything about you. Every part of you. And He knew just how you would take those parts and develop incredible strengths and frustrating challenges for yourself. He knew where you would flourish and where you would need help. And He offers an answer for every part of the personality He gave you.

God offers an answer for every part of the personality He gave you.

Have you taken tests or read books to discover your personality type? Which parts of the way God specifically made you bring you the most joy? List those here, along with reasons why you find joy in those things.

_____

_____

_____

_____

Read Philippians 1:3–11. Note that Paul, who wrote this letter to the church he started in Philippi, took great joy in the knowledge that God would keep working in the believers' hearts so they could live fully in the way He designed them. When you think about the way God made you, where do you see Him working to draw you closer to Him?

In the book of 1 Corinthians, Paul addresses some problems the church in Corinth was having. He encourages them to put their faith in God and His power rather than in human wisdom (1 Cor. 2:5), but then he acknowledges that wisdom is for the spiritually mature and the believers in Corinth were still quite immature in their faith (1 Cor. 3:1–2).

As the letter goes on, Paul presents his readers with more truth about God's design for their lives, challenging them to grow wiser and more spiritually mature. Likewise, in the book of Romans Paul urges believers to be transformed.

Read the following passages:

Romans 12:2

2 Corinthians 3:18

2 Corinthians 5:17

What do these passages indicate believers should be transformed from and transformed to? Where do you see yourself in the process of transformation? Are you closer to the beginning, the old ways? Or have you grown a lot, moving toward the new ways God has for you? Share your reflections here.

_____

_____

_____

_____

_____

_____

_____

Growing in our faith can be hard work. Even after we have believed in Jesus and promised to follow Him, we can struggle to leave our old ways behind. For example, we might understand that we are called to love our neighbor but still find ourselves gossiping. Perhaps we've read how love is patient and kind (1 Cor. 13:4) and that patience is a fruit of the Holy Spirit (Gal. 5:22–23), but at times we still let frustration and a short temper get the best of us. Or maybe, though we love God so very much—and we know that loving Him is the greatest commandment (Matt. 22:37–38)—we actually devote ourselves first to our career or family or hobbies or even ministries.

The good news is that God knows who we are and what we struggle with—and He doesn't need a personality quiz to figure it out. He made us, He knows us, and He loves us so much that He sent His only Son to save us. While we were still sinners, Jesus died for us (Rom. 5:8). But that's not all. Jesus triumphed over sin and death so He can empower us to do the same thing—even when that means overcoming our own sin nature and "the way we are."

Read Philippians 1:6 again. Rewrite it in your own words, replacing "you" with your name and describing the work God is doing in you.

_____

_____

_____

_____

Loving yourself as God's creation while also allowing Him to work in you and make you more like Jesus is not easy. How will you embrace your identity as a loved daughter of God while opening your heart to the work the Father wants to do in you this week?

_____

_____

_____

_____

Reflect on this prayer and make it your own today:

God, thank You for loving me—every part of me—quirks and flaws and all. I know that You have made me, and I know that sometimes I take Your creation and mess it up. Please forgive me. Give me wisdom to use every part of my heart and mind and soul to grow closer to You and find joy in being who You created me to be. Amen.

For you created my inmost being;
   you knit me together in my mother's womb.
I praise you because I am fearfully and wonderfully
      made;
   your works are wonderful,
   I know that full well.

Psalm 139:13–14 NIV

I remember the moment vividly. My husband and I were picking up a dining room set to refurbish, and the couple who was selling it asked what we did for a living. My husband talked about his career in the army, but I said, "I'm just an artist." Those words hit me even as they left my mouth. Instantly, I felt the sting in my heart. When we left, my husband asked me about it. I didn't know why it came out that way, but I told him it pained me to have said it.

One little word: *just.* Only four letters. But it was undervaluing and belittling, and it diminished the worth of who God made me to be. He has imprinted on my heart a beautiful, unique set of passions and abilities, and with one little word, I tossed that away. It felt like I had personally insulted Him.

Decades ago, when my classmates were deciding their career paths, I had something different on my heart. I wanted to attend art school. Not the most popular choice, and once I got there, I didn't feel like a typical art student. I felt so plain compared to my classmates. They couldn't even believe I grew up on a farm. But I knew I needed to embrace who God created me to be.

Then, even though I had taken many difficult steps to follow God on the incredible journey to becoming the person He created me to be, I stood there as an adult and diminished the worth of who I was. And it hurt.

We are never "just."

We are so much more than "just."

We are the incredible masterpieces of the Most High. He has created us as wonderfully unique individuals of great worth. We have been intricately designed for a purpose.

I seem to forget there has never been and will never be another person on this earth like me. I must not deny that distinctly beautiful person or the special loves, abilities, and passions that God planted inside me from the start.

When I stop using "just," I honor and embrace who He created me to be. And that does my heart good.

—JENNIFER UECKERT

Have you ever called yourself "just" anything? For example, "just a mom," "just a student," "just a nurse," "just a teacher." How did that make you feel, both in the moment and later?

Psalm 139 is the opposite of calling ourselves "just" anything. David was overjoyed at the fact that God made him. Add to that the understanding that God knows him so well and loves him so much, and it's no wonder David was moved to write poetry and songs to his Lord!

David knew very well how powerfully God could use someone who might have been considered small or unimportant. He began his life as "just the little brother," as well as "just a shepherd." But God didn't look at David through the lens of the world's values; He eventually used that young shepherd to lead a country.

As we discussed yesterday, God created each one of us and knows us intimately. And He is infinitely creative, giving every single person a unique set of skills and interests, so that when believers join with one another, we fit together perfectly as one body serving and glorifying God. That means your gifts, your passions, and everything else about you were given to you on purpose.

Read Ephesians 2:10. What good works were you created to do? It may be something God has placed on your heart during this study, or it may be something He has revealed to you previously. Take a few minutes to ask God this question and write down the answer.

When you describe yourself, what roles or characteristics do you use? Share those here. Next, read 1 John 3:1. What does this verse tell you about how God sees you? What is the most important role you have?

_____

_____

_____

_____

God did create us to do good works, and He made us unique and valuable. But more than any assignment or label we might take on, being a child of God is what's most significant about us. So even if we are not successful or impressive by the world's standards, we are still not "just" anything. We are children of God! God gives us all the significance we might crave by simply adopting us into His family.

> **God gives us all the significance we might crave by simply adopting us into His family.**

Read Ephesians 1:3–6. When did God decide to adopt you into His family? What qualifications did you have to meet or what accomplishments did you have to achieve?

_____

_____

God's love for us is not contingent on our qualifications or accomplishments. Before we ever did a single thing, He loved us and decided to save us and welcome us into His everlasting family.

David rejoices over God's love in Psalm 8 (and so many other psalms), praising God for who He is and then marveling that such an amazing, almighty God would bother with lowly humans. Though we are "just" humans, God loves us deeply.

In Luke 15, Jesus told a parable to explain how much He loves each one of us:

> If a man has a hundred sheep and one of them gets lost, what will he do? Won't he leave the ninety-nine others in the wilderness and go to search for the one that is lost until he finds it? And when he has found it, he will joyfully carry it home on his shoulders. When he arrives, he will call together his friends and neighbors, saying, "Rejoice with me because I have found my lost sheep." In the same way, there is more joy in heaven over one lost sinner who repents and returns to God than over ninety-nine others who are righteous and haven't strayed away! (vv. 3–7)

The shepherd in Jesus's story didn't say, "Oh, it's just one sheep. I have enough sheep. I won't worry about that one." No! He left those other sheep to find the one lost sheep. And that's exactly what the Good Shepherd—Jesus Christ—will do for you. You are never "just" one person, "just" an artist, "just" a woman, or "just" anything else. You are His beloved, the one He created, the one He loves, and the one He will leave all others to find and save.

Read Psalm 8 or Psalm 139 from beginning to end. Let the words sink into your heart as you consider how much God loves you "just" as you are. Share here how that knowledge brings you joy.

The things we believe about ourselves—the true ones from the Lord, the false ones from the world—can be hard to separate. And even when we know which ones are lies that diminish the work of God's hands and the love He has for us, we can struggle to let go of those labels we've been conditioned to accept. This week, when you find yourself believing you are "just" anything, what bold, brave truth can you turn to instead? Perhaps "I am a child of God!" or "I am fearfully and wonderfully made!" Write out the statement you'll cling to and refer back to it whenever you need a dose of courage and a perspective check this week.

Reflect on this prayer and make it your own today:

Heavenly Father, I want to take this time to praise You! You are so mighty and powerful and loving and kind. And so creative, Lord! You made me—and You made me wonderfully! Please forgive me for the times I've looked down on Your creation and judged it—judged myself—as less-than. I know I am Your child, and I want to live like it. Thank You, Father. Amen.

For you are all children of God through faith in Christ Jesus. And all who have been united with Christ in baptism have put on Christ, like putting on new clothes. There is no longer Jew or Gentile, slave or free, male and female. For you are all one in Christ Jesus. And now that you belong to Christ, you are the true children of Abraham. You are his heirs, and God's promise to Abraham belongs to you.

Galatians 3:26–29

Like a proud hen, our preschool director, Ms. Sharon, guided us, her precious little chicks, through the local market checkout lane. As an older preschooler, I was experiencing the thrill of a field trip to the store located only blocks away from the school. I felt so grown-up walking along downtown sidewalks while taking in all the sights, sounds, and smells.

Interacting with our community beyond the familiar home and family helps to shape notions about identity and how we fit in the world.

As we moved through the checkout line, mindful not to touch anything that did not belong to us, the cashier, who seemed very familiar with our preschool director, scanned all of our curious faces and said, "I didn't know that you were accepting *spots* at the preschool."

My intuition told me that something was wrong. Scrunching up her face to express confusion and disapproval, Ms. Sharon leaned in toward the cashier and asked what she was talking about. The cashier glared at me, the only Black child in the class, and then repeated herself: "I didn't know that you were accepting *spots*—" But this time, the cashier was firmly interrupted.

Ms. Sharon suddenly and gently shooed us past the cashier, attempting to shield us from her hurtful words. But I understood that Ms. Sharon was embarrassed by what the woman had said about me. Ms. Sharon then proceeded to reprimand the cashier. I don't remember what Ms. Sharon said, but decades later I can still see her face red with anger and feel her tense tone as she forced words through clenched white teeth and punctuated them with her wagging finger.

Though perplexed by this, by the time I entered elementary school I understood that the world had classified little Black girls like me as insignificant—not fully deserving of respect. Years of racist comments, the erasure of Black people from history lessons and religious imagery, and the misrepresentation of my ancestors' stories should have compounded to fortify a narrative of hopelessness. As a child, I should have been destroyed under the weight of society's toxic behavior.

But thankfully the world's narrative wasn't the only one I heard. One Sunday morning my Sunday school teacher read from Psalm 139: "I am fearfully and wonderfully made: Your works are wonderful" (v. 14). She then paraphrased it by saying, "God does not make junk. God creates everything and everyone with intention and purpose."

My young heart was overwhelmed with a joy that supersedes the world's interpretation of me. I am who God says I am.

—LUCRETIA BERRY

Have you ever felt ashamed of who you are or how you were made? Where do you think that shame comes from?

_____

_____

_____

_____

_____

Racism is not a new problem. Many Christians in the first century struggled to accept that God's love was now for everyone, not just the Jews. When Paul wrote to the believers in Galatia, he reminded them that, through the work of Jesus, every person who believed in Him was accepted as a child of God—no matter who they were, what they did, where they came from, or what they looked like (Gal. 3:26–29).

Jesus confirmed this foundational truth when He was asked to name the greatest commandment. In response, He explained that the entire law hangs on the commands to love God and to love others (Matt. 22:36–40). Later, when James reminds believers to love their neighbors as they love themselves, he refers to the original law from Leviticus 19:18 and to the words of Jesus. He even goes so far as to proclaim that "if you show favoritism, you sin and are convicted by the law as law-breakers" (James 2:8–9 NIV).

Have you ever been the victim of favoritism or racism? Have you been excluded or abused because of your identity? Write about one of those experiences. Then reread the last part of Lucretia's opening story. How do the words of Psalm 139:13–14 affirm who God says you are even when the world treats you unfairly?

Genesis 1:27 says that God created all people in His own image. (That includes you!) What does that tell you about what determines each person's worthiness to be loved?

The apostle Peter is famous for his bold expressions of faith, doubt, and everything in between. Unsurprisingly, when God revealed to him the truth about loving others equally, he didn't stay quiet. No, he told his friends about it, and they all rejoiced together in God's wisdom and love.

In Acts 10, Peter received a vision from God and an invitation from Cornelius, a Gentile believer in God, which made it clear to him that the gospel is for everyone, no matter their race, religion, or background. Peter accepted both the instruction and the invitation, saying to Cornelius and his family, "I see very clearly that God shows no favoritism. In every nation he accepts those who fear him and do what is right. This is the message of Good News for the people of Israel—that there is peace with God through Jesus Christ, who is Lord of all" (Acts 10:34–36).

> Can you think of a time when you have been guilty of showing favoritism to one group of people over another? How have you shown preference to or neglected a person because of their race, ethnicity, gender, career, marital status, age, economic status, or anything else other than their identity in Christ?

As we think about these hard things, may we take time today to seek healing—from the ways others have hurt us with their judgment or discrimination, *and* from the ways we have hurt others (and therefore God) by judging or discriminating.

If you have time, pause and pray about these things right now. Ask God for courage to process your past. Confess your sin. Receive God's healing truth.

God made every single part of you. Your blue eyes, your brown skin, the curve of your hips, your smile, the lilt of your voice, the tip of your nose, the size of your toes—every single part was intentionally designed by the most creative and loving God. And He loves you and commands every one of your brothers and sisters in Christ to love you as well.

But whether or not others see you the way your Creator does, God's vision of you, His beloved daughter, does not change. Despite every snub, every sneer, every invitation "lost in the mail," every phone that doesn't ring, every ugly name, every cold shoulder, the truth remains: you are a child of God, created, chosen, saved, and loved by Him. That is who you are. Let the joy of your true identity wash over you.

> You are a child of God, created, chosen, saved, and loved by Him. That is who you are.

Read this verse slowly: "But to all who did receive him, who believed in his name, he gave the right to become children of God" (John 1:12 ESV). Read it again and write down what thoughts or feelings come to mind. Now find a name tag, label, or sticky note and write, "I am a beloved child of God!" and stick it somewhere you will see it every day.

_____

_____

_____

_____

Believing a voice in a vision and then visiting a Roman centurion to share the gospel surely required a lot of courage from Peter. This week reflect on the truths that every person is made in the image of God (Gen. 1:27) and that everyone who calls on the name of the Lord will be saved (Rom. 10:13). How can these truths impact your life and bring you joy this week?

_____

_____

_____

Reflect on this prayer and make it your own today:

God, I'm so glad to know that You love me just as much as You love anyone else. I'm so thankful to know You created me in Your image! Please help me remember these truths when I'm treated badly—and please help me remember them when I choose how to treat others. Forgive me, Lord, for thinking that anyone's worth can be measured by anything other than their identity in You. I love You, Lord. Amen.

Let your light so shine before men, that they may see
your good works and glorify your Father in heaven.

Matthew 5:16 NKJV

I remember being called into my boss's office as a young employee and feeling worried that I had messed up. I sat down in front of his large executive desk as he closed the door. I was frantically going through my memory to find anything I might have done wrong.

As he sat down in his leather chair, he asked me in all seriousness, "Why are you so happy all the time?"

Taken aback, I wasn't even sure what he had just asked me.

"Happy all the time?" I asked.

"Yes," he said, a little frustrated with me. "You always have a smile on your face and seem happy no matter what happens. How do you do that?"

I knew my boss struggled with down days. He had grown up in a very religious home based on works. He tried to be kind to those he led and to love others, but he never acted like he enjoyed his life or was very happy.

I had prayed for over a year for him to have a real relationship with Jesus, to know he was unconditionally loved and to feel free to be happy without guilt. Here was my open door to share the secret of my joy. That day we had a surprising conversation about my faith in Jesus.

If I hadn't allowed the joy in my life to spread to my face, would my boss have asked me about my heart? A smile is a gesture of vulnerability and can make others curious about the Jesus we long to share.

I wonder if the way we live makes a life with Jesus look like a joyous adventure or an unhappy religion.

Sometimes the people I meet who don't have a saving relationship with Jesus seem happier than those who do. That isn't the way God intended us to live after experiencing eternal freedom from sin and unconditional love.

Let's be women of Jesus, living a life that shows others we are His ambassadors and are promised joy with His Spirit so that people will pause to ask us why we can be so happy in the middle of this chaotic world.

—STEPHANIE BRYANT

Has anyone ever commented about the joy you have? What was your response? How do you recognize joy in other people's lives?

_____

_____

_____

_____

In what is known as the Sermon on the Mount (Matt. 5–7), Jesus preached to an enormous crowd. One of the first lessons He taught was about the believer's role in the world. Using metaphors of salt and light, He emphasized that we are to be so full of God's love that those who don't know Him are drawn to Him through us (5:13–16). Like light in a dark night, our joy in the Lord should shine so brightly that people not only will wonder where it comes from but will want to know how they can have that same joy.

Shining brightly? With contagious joy? If we look around at a lot of believers (or if we take an honest look at ourselves), that might seem impossible or at least uncommon. But theologian A. W. Tozer affirms what Jesus preached: "The people of God ought to be the happiest people in all the wide world! People should be coming to us constantly and asking the source of our joy and delight."[1]

How do others describe you and your temperament? If you don't believe they'd call you happy, do you think that's because you don't feel joy or because you don't express it?

Where can you find more delight in your life and in the Lord? Read the following verses to help you answer that question:

Psalm 37:4

Psalm 119:33–35

Jeremiah 9:24

The book of Acts tells the story of the early church. Though the followers of Jesus were opposed and even persecuted, their numbers grew exponentially as the gospel spread. A short but powerful description of the church found in Acts 2 explains part of why so many were drawn to this new way.

Read Acts 2:42–47 and take note of the last two sentences: "They ate their food with joyful and sincere hearts, praising God and enjoying the favor of all the people. Every day the Lord added to their number those who were being saved." The members of that first church were living in true community—eating together, worshiping together, sharing their possessions. They found great joy in sharing life and pointing one another to Christ. Their joy was, in fact, contagious. And many people were saved because of it.

What joy the believers must have felt at that news. Their numbers multiplied, and so did their joy. What a cycle!

Does this mean we are expected to act happy no matter what? Is the fate of the world—or more accurately, the salvation of the lost—dependent on how much we love life? Not exactly. Rather, it means that when we are filled with delight in the Lord, our joy will be a light that shines on the people around us and points them back to God.

> **When we are filled with delight in the Lord, our joy will be a light that shines on the people around us and points them back to God.**

And why wouldn't you want that?

God knows that some situations and seasons in life are hard. In fact, Jesus promises that we will certainly have trouble in this world (John 16:33). But He also promises to help us through it (Ps. 46:1), and even in that we can find great joy. Jesus never asks us to pretend like everything is great and easy in order to attract people to God. But He does tell us to find joy in all circumstances (James 1:2–4), knowing that it will certainly intrigue those around us and give us the opportunity to share exactly where we find our hope and resilient joy.

Even during a time of persecution, the early Christians found great joy in God's love and in fellowship with one another. What are you finding so much joy in right now that other people take notice? If you're in a place where it's hard to find joy, read James 1:2–4 again. Ask God to give you the courage to "count it all joy"—whatever your "it" may be today.

_____

_____

_____

_____

Read 1 Peter 3:14–15. Prepare yourself to give an answer for the hope you have. Write down what you could say to someone who asks where your joy comes from.

_____

_____

_____

_____

Reflect on this prayer and make it your own today:

Dear God, I want to be a woman who is unashamedly filled with so much joy that people can't help but ask where it comes from. But I know I'm not always this woman. Forgive me, Lord. Remind me daily of the joy I have in knowing You love me enough not only to die for me but to send Your Spirit to continue to guide me. Increase my delight today that others might see Your light in me and ask why. Amen.

So God created human beings in his own image.
  In the image of God he created them;
    male and female he created them. . . .

Then God looked over all he had made, and he saw that
it was very good!

Genesis 1:27, 31

Some days I look at my thirty-eight-year-old face in the mirror and wonder how I could possibly be attractive, even to my husband. I notice the pores that never shrank, the blotchiness that makes my cheeks look flushed (but not in a cute way), the fold lines on my neck I wish I could iron out. I see my protruding belly in the mirror and swear I must look thirty weeks pregnant, and wonder if I might regain some of my youthfulness if I could just stop eating whatever I want to.

So I pull on my tummy-tucking jeggings and wear a tunic-length shirt to hide the bulges. I patch up the acne scars and dark bags under my eyes with a stick of concealer and blend in another layer of liquid foundation. It's nearly impossible to find the right shade for my skin color, so two are often better than one. I curl my stubbornly straight eyelashes, inevitably pulling some of them out, and I wear mascara to give the illusion that my almond-shaped eyes are bigger than they really are.

When God made human beings and finished His work of creation, He looked at all He had made and called it very good. Everything was unaltered, natural, and pure. Nothing was hidden, covered, or shamed, because everything in its most basic form was already very good.

I hardly ever say that what I see in the mirror is very good, and I know there will still be days when I slather on my makeup, curl my eyelashes, and tuck in my belly, hoping to see someone new looking back at me.

I don't have a face or body the world might deem pretty or sexy, and as time passes, even what seems decent now will soon fade away. But I'm slowly learning to respect what is mine—my almond eyes, my flat nose, my round face—and I'm speaking new words over myself:

You are very good.

—GRACE P. CHO

What do you see when you look in the mirror? How does your appearance—and your opinion of it—affect how you believe God sees you?

_____

_____

_____

_____

Earlier this week we talked about David, who began his life as "just" a young shepherd. In addition to showing us how to rejoice in the Lord, David is an excellent example of how God is more concerned with a person's inner beauty than their outward appearance. As the Old Testament prophet Samuel searched for Israel's new king, God guided him to the house of a man named Jesse. Samuel assumed that Eliab, Jesse's oldest son, was the future leader God had in mind. Instead, God told him, "Don't judge by his appearance or height, for I have rejected him. The LORD doesn't see things the way you see them. People judge by outward appearance, but the LORD looks at the heart" (1 Sam. 16:7). In fact, God rejected all seven of David's older, stronger brothers and then pointed Samuel to the young shepherd. What a surprise that must have been—for Samuel, for David, for David's family, and even for us reading the story today!

Now, David is described as having "a fine appearance and handsome features" (1 Sam. 16:12 NIV). Why then did God point out that appearance is not important? Because He knew that physical beauty fades quickly and the world's standards of beauty change frequently, but the strength of our character endures. God's plan for our lives isn't dictated or limited by our physical bodies. We see this in His words about David as well as in the life of Moses.

Read Exodus 4:10–12. What physical trait was Moses worried about? Was God concerned with this problem? How does God's response change your perception of your own less-than-perfect body, appearance, or skills?

Read Proverbs 31:30 and write it here. As you think about the value God places on our physical appearance versus how much He values our heart, do you feel encouraged or discouraged?

_____

_____

_____

_____

While God clearly places much more value on our insides than our outsides, He *is* the artist who designed our physical bodies. He made us in His image and then, when He sat back to evaluate His work, He said it was "very good" (Gen. 1:31). God never looks at us and thinks, *Well, if only I'd made her eyes a little bigger or her legs a little thinner or her hair a little smoother . . .* No! He looks at us and calls us very good.

Song of Solomon is a book of the Bible that describes the love between a husband and wife, but it also illustrates the great, passionate love God has for His people. That love includes admiring His people's beauty, with kind words such as, "You are altogether beautiful, my love; there is no flaw in you" (Song of Sol. 4:7 ESV).

The same joy Solomon's bride must have felt at hearing those words is available to us if we receive them as God's truth spoken tenderly over us. God the Creator, the One who made the mountains and the oceans and the stars and every sunset and sunrise, also made you and finds you "altogether beautiful." The flaws you see? He doesn't. He sees His beloved, cherished, and chosen daughter—perfectly made in His image.

Look up Song of Solomon 4:7 in multiple translations. (You can do this at BibleGateway.com or by using a Bible app.) Now write out the verse below and replace "my dearest," "my love," or "my darling" with your

own name. Bonus: write it again on something you can stick to your
mirror and read often.

_____

_____

_____

_____

_____

In our visually oriented society it can be hard not to feel critical of
our appearance. This world offers no shortage of physical standards
that are impossible to meet, leaving us perpetually grasping for something we will never reach. Insecurity about our appearance is a reasonable response, but it means we have be-
lieved that what the world says matters
more than what the Lord says. The better, healthier, holier response is to turn
our eyes away from our own reflection
and toward God.

> **When we gaze upon God and then see ourselves through His eyes, we can't help but feel love and joy for the person He's made us to be.**

When we gaze upon Him and then
see ourselves through His eyes, we can't help but feel love and joy for
the person He's made us to be. As David—yes, the same David!—wrote
in Psalm 34:5, "Those who look to [God] are radiant, and their faces
shall never be ashamed" (ESV).

Read Isaiah 43:1–7. According to this passage, what has God done for
you? How does He see you?

_____

_____

_____

Looking at ourselves with affection rather than criticism can be a challenge. How will you courageously find joy in God's creation when you face yourself in the mirror this week?

Reflect on this prayer and make it your own today:

God, thank You for understanding how damaging this world can be to my sense of value and worth. Thank You for telling me over and over in Scripture that You made me perfectly and that You think I'm beautiful. I know my heart matters more than my hair or hips. When I'm hard on myself, remind me to turn my gaze to You. Continue to make me more like You every day so that I reflect my Creator inside and out. Thank You, Lord. I love You. Amen.

joy in the good times

Let them praise his name with dancing
and make music to him with tambourine and lyre.

Psalm 149:3 CSB

In the fall of 2011, we discovered our daughter, Faith, had a broken neck. Before and after her precarious but successful corrective surgery, Faith endured strict limitations on her mobility. For months, she reluctantly kept her physical activity to a minimum. Playing on the jungle gym during recess at school? Nope. Riding her bike around the neighborhood? Double nope. Faith couldn't even go down the stairs at home without one of us holding her hand.

And if you think this was a difficult period for our independent, doesn't-like-to-sit-still girl, then you'd be right.

After adhering to this regimen for months, the glorious appointment arrived when the neurosurgeon gave Faith the green light to abandon the neck brace and begin selective physical activity. I can still see her face taking in the news—her grin a country mile wide—as her pastel world turned jewel-toned.

On the drive home, we laughed and sang a chorus of "Praise God from Whom All Blessings Flow." For dinner, I made Faith's favorites: hot dogs, apple slices, and macaroni and cheese. Afterwards, I flipped on the radio while we cleared the table and swept the floors. As one of our favorite country songs twirled through speakers and around our dining room table, I looked up from the kitchen sink to find Faith twirling along with the music.

My mouth dropped open at the scene before me, soapy suds dripping from my hands hanging midair. Because while I had hoped and prayed my girl would dance again, I couldn't picture it till that moment when I saw God's grace in her graceful motion, my quiet hope now plainly visible.

We danced in royal fashion like we owned the night, right there in our linoleum and Formica kitchen. I stopped long enough to mark the moment in my heart: *Today we saw the hope of the Lord, the giver of fresh starts.*

That was several years ago, but every time I hear that song, I dance and remember that moment as a promise of hope when the difficult we-don't-know-how-this-will-end turned into something we could see in plain sight.

My daughter still has residual effects from her broken neck. She is healed but not completely whole physically, so certain activities will always be off-limits for her. However, much *is* possible. Beauty surrounds her, and there are endless reasons to be grateful as we celebrate God's faithfulness, both seen and yet-to-be-seen.

And because of this, we dance.

—KRISTEN STRONG

When was the last time you were so overjoyed that you found yourself singing, dancing, laughing, or crying?

King David knew a thing or two about dancing in worship before the Lord. In 2 Samuel 6, we read about Israel's great celebration after recovering the ark of the covenant. The ark, which symbolized God's special presence in the midst of His people, had been held in captivity by Israel's enemies, the Philistines. Now they were bringing it back to Jerusalem and rejoicing over its repossession. They sang, danced, and played instruments of all kinds in their celebration. As David led the parade, he was "leaping and dancing before the LORD" (v. 16).

When we experience God's love and mercy toward us in a meaningful way, when we focus on His faithfulness and kindness, we can't help but celebrate and praise Him!

> **When we focus on God's faithfulness and kindness, we can't help but celebrate and praise Him!**

Of course, not everyone loves dancing, even when we're at our most uninhibited and overjoyed. We don't need to be talented dancers to worship the Lord. Just dance! But if you're so uncoordinated or self-conscious that being forced to dance would steal your joy rather than express it, that's okay too. God is honored by many different forms of rejoicing. In 2 Samuel 6 we see God's people playing musical instruments, gathering together, offering sacrifices, wearing special clothing, dancing, shouting, and feasting—all as expressions of the joy they found in the Lord.

Read 2 Samuel 6:1–19 in the NIV translation. Take note of verses 5 and 14. How do these verses say that David and the Israelites celebrated?

_____

_____

_____

_____

_____

What does dancing with "all your might" look like for you? If you're not comfortable with dancing, what else could you do to express your abundant joy in the Lord? Does anything keep you from doing that?

David's joy was increased by his long wait to welcome the ark of the covenant to his home. Joy intensified by a delay is an experience echoed by so many of God's children who endured excruciatingly long waits to see God's promises come true (like Abraham, who waited decades for God to give him the promised son).

Perhaps, like the Israelites and David and even Kristen's daughter, you've experienced joy made greater and deeper because of the wait that preceded it. Like the time you finally got the job or made the friend or kicked the habit. Most of us have gone through a desert season. Maybe you're in that season right now.

Has God ever answered your prayers after a long wait? How did the time you spent waiting for God to change circumstances or work in your heart affect your joy and the way you celebrated?

David celebrated with such wild abandon that his own wife, Michal, scorned his behavior as vulgar (2 Sam. 6:16, 20). It's true that Michal and David had quite a bit of baggage between them. But aside from that, it's worth noting that sometimes our celebration and worship might be misunderstood or criticized.

Did that stop David? No. Should that stop us? Of course not. Just like we talked about in week 2, rejoicing with courage means we respond to God honestly and in whatever way He created us to rejoice. Sometimes that might mean quietly singing hymns or praying silently; other times it might mean shouting and singing at the top of our lungs.

When Michal criticized David's dancing, he replied, "I was dancing before the LORD. . . . Yes, and I am willing to look even more foolish than this, even to be humiliated in my own eyes!" (2 Sam. 6:21–22).

When others question our exuberance or when we doubt ourselves, let's say with David, "My worship is for the Lord, so it doesn't matter what anyone else thinks of me." And then, let's dance!

Take one more look at 2 Samuel 6. Count how many times the phrase "before the Lord" is used. What is the significance of these words and their frequency?

_____

_____

_____

_____

_____

_____

Are you willing to look foolish or feel uncomfortable for the sake of praising God and experiencing His joy? How might seeing believers live a life of exuberant joy help people see Christianity differently?

_____

_____

_____

_____

_____

_____

Reflect on this prayer and make it your own today:

Lord, so many times You make me want to dance and sing and shout and let all my inhibitions go so I can fully express how much joy You give! Fill me with courage to embrace that joy and celebrate with all my might before You. And when life is a little less thrilling, give me eyes to see all the ways I can rejoice in everyday blessings. Amen.

Because of the LORD's faithful love
we do not perish,
for his mercies never end.
They are new every morning;
great is your faithfulness!

Lamentations 3:22–23 CSB

My heart was just beginning to heal from deep community-related wounds when I was diagnosed with a brain tumor. After months of symptoms, questions, and tests, we finally had an answer. It seemed that everyone around me held their breath, anticipating fear or a wave of emotion. But the most overwhelming peace swept over me and covered me like a warm blanket on a cold night.

I was seventeen and grateful. After a year of loss, a year of watching so much crumble, a year of walking through a valley with no mountaintop in sight, I knew one thing for certain: God would be faithful. His peace filled me, and He promised joy would come in the morning. I couldn't see it yet, couldn't feel it, but a promise is a promise, and God keeps every single one He makes.

A few days after receiving the news that would rewrite my story, I checked in to the hospital for brain surgery. Without a bow to tie everything up nicely, I began to share my story from the valley. The journey was difficult but the choice was easy: if God could receive the glory, then I wanted to tell the story.

The golf-ball-sized tumor was removed and my body began to heal, but the holes in my heart remained. I can't point to a surgery date on the calendar, and it was far from a quick fix, but over time, God's relentless love pursued me, leading me back to His bride, the very community that had hurt me so deeply.

He is the God who turns tests into testimonies and messes into messages, the God who breathes life into what seems too far gone, the One who brings beauty from ashes and mends what has shattered. There will be struggles and valleys, brain tumors and broken hearts. We may stand among the ruins, but He will not leave us there. It may be dark and the night may be long, but sooner or later dawn will break.

Joy comes with the morning.

—KAITLYN BOUCHILLON

Have you experienced healing—physical, emotional, spiritual, or relational? Who did you credit for that healing? How did you show your thanks?

_____

_____

_____

_____

_____

One mark of a rich relationship with God is finding joy in the Lord *before* seeing a happy ending. The Old Testament prophet Jeremiah demonstrated this. The book of Jeremiah records his warning to God's people, predicting that the consequences of their rebellion would be the devastation and loss of their homeland. Jeremiah felt their pain deeply and showed extreme empathy, as recorded in the book of

Lamentations, but he also rejoiced in God's great compassion for His people.

Even when writing a book dedicated to expressing sorrow, Jeremiah still held on to hope. From the depths of his despair, Jeremiah remembered that God would not leave him and that his struggles would not last forever. He rejoiced preemptively, trusting that one way or another God would still rescue His children.

One mark of a rich relationship with God is finding joy in the Lord before seeing a happy ending.

Read Lamentations 3:22–26. What does it mean to believe the Lord's mercies never end? How has God's faithful love kept you from harm or despair?

Read Jeremiah 29:11–14. God gave Jeremiah a message for the Israelites. Even though life was going to get real hard real soon because of their stubborn disobedience, God promised that He would not abandon them forever and would eventually rescue them again. Have you ever been expectant for God's rescue while still facing a big problem? If so, how did that perspective affect you?

Isaiah was another messenger tasked with warning the nations of Judah and Israel about the dire consequences they would face if they continued to turn away from the Lord. But even in His anger and disappointment, God still expressed His great love for His people, reminding them of the abundant blessings He wanted to give them.

In Isaiah 43, God implores His children to come back to Him. Read it like a plea from a loving Father: *Don't you know how much I love you? You don't have to be afraid! I will protect you, no matter what you go through. And even though things are hard, they're going to get so much better. I'm working on something brand-new for you, and I can't wait for you to see it!*

God isn't looking the other way or twiddling His thumbs while we are suffering. Instead, He's working all things together for our good and His glory. So when we're hurt by our closest friends, when we're diagnosed with cancer, when we're served divorce papers or a termination notice, when we answer the middle-of-the-night phone call and the news is as bad as we feared, God hasn't left us. He is still with us, and He promises that He's doing a new thing. And that is cause for joy—even while we're still in the valley.

What do the following proverbs teach you about God's plans? If you believe these things are true, how does that change your outlook?

Proverbs 3:5–6

Proverbs 16:9

Proverbs 19:21

The psalms are like an emotional roller coaster. From the depths of despair to the summit of celebration, the psalmists are brutally honest about their feelings. We can conclude then that God welcomes all of it—our sorrow, our anger, our desperation, our tentative hope, our deep faith, our wild delight, our great love and gratitude. And we can see through the psalms that the joy we desire and that God offers will always be found again.

So why not start celebrating now?

Even when we are walking through the valley of the shadow of death (Ps. 23:4), we can know the relief of God's presence. Even when we are facing the hardest circumstances, we can prepare our heart for the new thing God is doing and start finding joy in His plan now. Even when we can't see it. Even when it's not what we expected. Even then, we can rejoice in God!

Read Psalm 28. Though the song begins with David desperately crying out to the Lord for help, he eventually says, "My heart is filled with joy. I burst out in songs of thanksgiving" (v. 7). What can you praise God for, right now, in the middle of any challenge you're facing? Make a list and repeat it often—to yourself and to God.

Who needs to hear your right-now, work-in-progress story of praise? Who can you courageously share that joy with?

_____

_____

_____

_____

_____

Reflect on this prayer and make it your own today:

God, thank You for loving me so much that I can trust Your love even when life feels unbearable. Please open my eyes to all the blessings You've given me, and give me the courage to believe completely in You and Your good plans. I want to celebrate what You're doing in my life even before I know the end of the story, because You are the Author of my life, Lord, and I trust You. Thank You. I love You! Amen.

But let all who take refuge in you be glad;
  let them ever sing for joy.
Spread your protection over them,
  that those who love your name may rejoice in you.

Psalm 5:11 NIV

Last year my family celebrated my mom's twentieth year of being a breast cancer survivor. We celebrated every one of those 7,300 gifted-to-us days with pink everything, loud laughter, tearful stories, and being together.

The week before our party, I attended the funeral of a friend who punched metastatic breast cancer in the face for eight years, right up until the end. Hundreds of us gathered to celebrate her life through our tears. With such a different kind of celebration so fresh in my mind, the celebration for my mom was even deeper and more meaningful than I'd expected it to be.

We have today, which means we have a chance to celebrate.

So do it. Celebrate—whatever you want, whenever you want. Put up all the autumn decorations. Eat the cake. Throw the party. Put up your Christmas tree. Lean into celebration whenever you can, because there is extraordinary in every single one of our plain old everydays, and each one of them deserves to be celebrated.

The God we celebrate and praise created each of us with unique likes and things that bring us joy, and I'm pretty sure He wants us to lean into them. "The glory of God is man fully alive." Those words of Irenaeus resonate in my year-round Christmas-loving heart because celebrating holidays both big and small is part of who God made me to be. I hope it brings Him glory when I live that out, operating in who I am by His design.

When it comes to celebrations, you do you. Celebrate in the way that's most meaningful for you, and don't let anyone tell you there's a better or different or right way to do it.

Whatever brings joy to you and glory to God, do that—during the holidays and all your days.

—ANNA RENDELL

Think of a time when you celebrated in an unusual way—either in what you were celebrating or how you celebrated. What about that experience gave you the most joy?

_____

_____

_____

_____

_____

The Old Testament book of Ecclesiastes examines life apart from God. Its author comes away with a pretty grim outlook, emphasizing the pointless nature of living a life focused on earthly matters and separated from our Creator. However, toward the end of the book, the author concludes that God is in control and we really don't know what will happen (Eccles. 9:1). With that in mind, he encourages readers to live life fully.

Read Ecclesiastes 9:7–9 in *The Message*. In this passage the author describes our "precarious life." Other versions translate that phrase as "meaningless days." And while that might sound like a bleak (albeit accurate) outlook, it simply acknowledges that the only thing we know for sure is that this life is temporary. With that in mind, the author urges readers to enjoy this short life while we can. In other words, *You're still here? Let's celebrate!*

Rejoicing can feel tricky at times. Maybe you're not quite out of the woods, but you still feel joy about what God has done so far and what you trust Him to do in the future. Maybe others are hurting while you are experiencing a time of abundance, or perhaps it seems that others see your gifts or success as something small and unworthy of great celebration. God doesn't minimize any of our emotions. As He shows us throughout Scripture, He values the small and the overlooked, and He wants us to seek and share joy.

Read Ecclesiastes 3:1–14. We're told that there is a time (or "season" or "occasion," depending on which translation you read) for everything. With this passage in mind, is there ever a good time not to rejoice in the Lord? Why or why not?

_____

_____

_____

_____

_____

Read John 10:10. What does an abundant life look like? If you believe Jesus wants to give you an abundant life, how does that affect the way you approach celebrating in the day-to-day?

_____

_____

_____

_____

_____

When Paul writes to the church in Ephesus and gives them instructions for living "worthy of the calling" (Eph. 4:1 CSB), he tells them to make the most of every opportunity (Eph. 5:15–16). And while he does give a list of don'ts, he also explains what making the most of every opportunity looks like: "Be filled with the Spirit, speaking to one another with psalms, hymns, and songs from the Spirit. Sing and make music from your heart to the Lord, always giving thanks to God the Father for everything, in the name of our Lord Jesus Christ" (Eph. 5:18–20 NIV).

At the end of the day (or at the end of our life), we all want to be described as someone who found joy in every season and situation and thanked God through all of it. We all want to be part of our family and friends' "time to dance" and "time to laugh" (Eccles. 3:4).

Whether our personality leans toward huge, raucous parties or small, intimate gatherings, toward spontaneous celebrations or carefully planned events, it is good for us to purposefully rejoice in what God has done, is doing, and will do in our lives. It's good to do it now, to do it often, to do it in exactly the way He's created us to.

What can you celebrate with all of your heart—right now or this week (Col. 3:23)? What could that celebration look like, and who could you invite to share in your joy?

_____

_____

_____

While teaching His followers on the Mount of Olives, Jesus told the story of a manager who entrusted his employees with different amounts of money before he left on a trip. When the manager returned, he was pleased with how two of the employees had handled his money wisely, but he was displeased with a third employee who had mishandled his money (Matt. 25:14–30).

If we understand this parable to illustrate God's relationship with us, we can see that God is concerned with how we care for the blessings He gives us. Do we hide them away, afraid He'll never give us more? Do we ignore them, ashamed or resentful that we didn't receive the same gift as someone else? Or do we take what we're given— our life, our salvation—and embrace it? Do we share and multiply its goodness by rejoicing in it with others?

> **Let's thank God for every bit of this life He's given us. Let's rejoice always. Never mind what the neighbors think; it's time to celebrate the Lord!**

James 1:17 reminds us that every good gift, big or small, comes from the Lord. *Every* gift. Let's thank God for every bit of this life He's given us. Let's rejoice always. Never mind what the neighbors think; it's time to celebrate the Lord!

Read Matthew 5:14–16. What does this passage tell you might be a result of your joy in the Lord? Can you think of a time when your choice to celebrate, perhaps in an unusual or surprising way, led to conversations about God and His blessings?

So many obstacles get in the way of our celebrating. We think we don't have enough time or money or friends with room in their schedules. We're afraid people might see us as silly or wasteful or presumptuous. We're not sure that our enthusiasm and gratitude will last or even matter to anyone else. But God says, "Rejoice!" So let's rejoice! How will you push through obstacles to make the choice to celebrate with God and in God this week?

_____

_____

_____

_____

Reflect on this prayer and make it your own today:

O God, thank You for giving me so many reasons to celebrate! Just like Psalm 16 says, my whole being rejoices! Forgive me for the times I've restrained my joy or even hidden it away. When I feel awkward or unsure about celebrating, Lord, please give me courage. Make me brave enough to sing praises to You for everything You've done, everything You're doing right now, and everything You're going to do. Thank You for all of it, God. I love You! Amen.

Let the heavens be glad, and the earth rejoice!
    Let the sea and everything in it shout his praise!
Let the fields and their crops burst out with joy!
    Let the trees of the forest sing for joy.

Psalm 96:11–12

Tall pines stood around me, bearing witness to the smile stretched across my face. The campground was alive with morning noises—bacon sizzling on outdoor skillets, kids laughing louder than they would at home. I watched a bright blue-chested bird perch on a branch heavy with pine cones while two hummingbirds zipped around in a magical dance. I sipped slowly on my steamy coffee.

Everything is better in the mountains.

This was my family's favorite week—when we (mostly) unplug, enjoy nature, and soak up lots of time just being together. With fresh air in my lungs and no alarm to wake me up except for the loud whispers of three excited kids, it was easy to start each day with gratitude in my heart. I thanked God for crackling campfires, family cornhole tournaments, and sunny trails just waiting for the happy thud of hiking boots.

Thank You, God, for seeing our need for a break from ordinary routine.

One afternoon I sat on a huge log at the far end of our campsite. My husband was out jogging, and my boys were building an epic fort. In the stillness of the moment—no one needing me, no task demanding to be done—I felt the nearness of God's presence.

With the sun on my back and the gift of time, I was flooded with awareness for all the ways God had answered so many prayers. So I was a little surprised by what the Spirit whispered to my heart next: *Give thanks for the gifts you didn't ask for. Praise Me for answers you never prayed for.* Looking around, I realized that this moment was forged in blessings I never requested, which magnified my joy even more.

I didn't ask God for a husband who loved camping, yet He gave me a partner with a shared appreciation for fresh-air wonder. I never thought to ask God for in-laws who would be generous with their time and treasure, yet that's what God gave me in two people willing to loan us their beautiful trailer for a week every summer.

What joy to soak in the simple blessings of mountain air and the God who sees the needs we have today and the ones yet to come.

—BECKY KEIFE

Look around. What blessing has God given that you never thought to ask for?

_____

_____

_____

_____

_____

"Shout for joy to the Lord!" the Bible tells us over and over.

That's nice, we might think as we consider those passages. Then we move on to what feels like the weightier, more relevant, more important stuff of our faith—seeking our "real" purpose and significance, healing our divisions, figuring out how to care for the poor and the planet, and just trying to make it through the day with our sanity intact. It doesn't leave much energy or room in our schedules to "shout for joy," does it?

Yet the Bible repeatedly states, "Rejoice! Rejoice! Rejoice!"

With the call to rejoice commanded so often throughout Scripture, it indicates the Lord is telling us that actively choosing and expressing joy is significant to our focus and essential to our well-being as believers. If we want our faith to grow, if we want to draw nearer to our Savior, then we must engage in the spiritual practice of celebration by digging into our courageous joy. When we do, we'll discover it's a vital part of the rhythm of faith and life.

Are you surprised by how many times the Bible talks about joy? Flip to the back of your Bible, and in the concordance or index look up the words "joy" and "rejoice." You might also look for "joyful," "joyous," "rejoicing," "rejoiced," and other variants of the word. (If your Bible doesn't have a concordance or index, you can search those words on BibleGateway.com or in a Bible app.) How many mentions can you find? What does this tell you about God's priority regarding our joy?

Read Psalm 96 and then answer the following questions:

- What "glorious deeds" or "wondrous works" could you tell others that God has done for you (v. 3)?

_____

_____

_____

- How does our praise—or our joy—glorify God (v. 8)?

_____

_____

_____

- How does nature rejoice and praise God (vv. 11–12)?

_____

_____

_____

Perhaps part of God's purpose in pointing us to joy again and again is to help us appreciate what we have while we have it. And perhaps that is how nature can honor and glorify Him—by reminding us of the Creator's majesty and compelling us to express our joy.

Throughout Scripture we're given examples of how to rejoice in the Lord, and often it involves praising God for His creation. Even in Psalm 69, where David is asking God for protection from his enemies, he ends by praising God and inviting all of nature to join him: "Let heaven and earth praise him, the seas and everything that moves in them" (v. 34 ESV).

When we're mindful of God's creation, we stay mindful of Him—which means our joy is a consistent foundation of our life rather than a fleeting emotion we miss when it's gone.

We don't all live near mountains or beaches or even wide-open fields. Not everyone can spend a few days at a campground or drive to a state park for a few hours. But no matter where you live, you can spot something that God made. A sliver of blue sky between buildings, a baby's belly laugh, a heart-stopping thunderstorm, a plant on a coworker's desk, a bold squirrel outside your window—all of these things testify to God's creativity and beauty, to His sense of humor and His great power. We're surrounded by blessings, no matter what our specific surroundings look like.

> **When we're mindful of God's creation, we stay mindful of Him—which means our joy is a consistent foundation of our life rather than a fleeting emotion we miss when it's gone.**

Read this Old Testament prayer out loud:

You alone are the LORD. You made the heavens, even the highest heavens, and all their starry host, the earth and all that is on it, the seas and all that is in them. You give life to everything, and the multitudes of heaven worship you. (Neh. 9:6 NIV)

What is your favorite way to enjoy God's creation? Write out your praise for the beauty of what God has made.

God's creation is so incredible that it won't allow us to forget or ignore or neglect Him. Regardless of our busy schedules, our concrete kingdoms, our determination to go, do, and be more, God's blessings are always present, waiting for us to take notice, to give thanks, to find joy. When we stay mindful, grateful, and joyful, we'll never again need to say, "I didn't know what I had until it was gone."

In Becky's story, she marvels that God knows her so well that He gave her gifts she didn't even know she needed. Read Psalm 139. What does that tell you about how well God knows what you need and what will bring you joy?

As you continue to meditate on the words of the psalms from today's study, how will you find joy in small or unexpected gifts around you?

Reflect on this prayer and make it your own today:

*Lord, You are so creative! Thank You for placing me in this
exact spot of Your creation right now. Please open my eyes to all
the ways You are caring for me and blessing me, even in ways
I never thought to ask for or imagined could be possible. Thank
You, God. You bring me so much joy, and I'm grateful. Amen.*

The LORD your God is among you,
a warrior who saves.
He will rejoice over you with gladness.
He will be quiet in his love.
He will delight in you with singing.

Zephaniah 3:17 CSB

Mommy, what do cows like to do?"

"I don't know. What?" I reply.

"They like to go to the mooooovies."

My kids burst into laughter and immediately proceed to explain the joke to me. They want to make sure I understand it as much as they enjoy telling it.

I'm delighted more by their joy than by the joke. It emanates from their faces, starting with the sparkle in their eyes and spreading to their wide smiles. They tilt their heads back, laughter bubbling up from their bellies, and they remind me of my favorite painting of Jesus laughing. It's unlike most paintings of Jesus, which usually portray Him as serious, and something about His joyous face seems so human to me.

We know the Jesus who rebuked the Pharisees and taught in synagogues, the One who amazed people with His miracles and fed thousands with a few loaves and fish, the One who died on the cross and rose again. We may have images of these moments etched into our memories from paintings we've seen or pictures from our childhood Bibles. But I remember all of those pictures depicting Jesus as stoic and unapproachable. Perhaps the artists were going for holy and divine, which He is, but I wonder if we don't know how to relate to the joy of the Lord because we don't often see pictures of Jesus laughing or enjoying a meal with His disciples.

The thing is, joy and delight *are* holy and divine. They come from God. The painting of Jesus laughing makes Him more human to me, but perhaps it goes the other way too. My children bear God's divine image through their humor and head-tilting laughter, and I can choose to enter into the holy space of joy with every silly joke they tell me.

—GRACE P. CHO

When was the last time you belly laughed or laughed so hard you cried? What was it that delighted you so much?

Sometimes we oversimplify the two parts of the Bible, labeling the Old Testament as harsh or even boring while pointing to the New Testament as the more loving, relatable half of God's Word. But while the Old Testament is full of battles and wars and armies and kings, it's also a love letter. Every time God sends a prophet to warn the Israelites to turn back to Him, He tells them how much joy He finds in them and how He longs to bring that same joy into their lives rather than judgment.

In the book of Zephaniah, the prophet urges the people of Judah to turn back to God. He warns them in great detail of the devastation and pain that will come if they do not repent. But then he offers hope by reminding them of God's faithful love and His promise of redemption. He tells them God loves them so much that He rejoices over them with gladness and singing (Zeph. 3:17).

The prophet Isaiah also shares God's truth with the people of Judah. Isaiah tells them what will happen to their nation if they don't return to God. He explains why trusting the Lord and obeying His commands are a must—and that there will be consequences for ignoring those commands. But he also communicates the Lord's deep love for His people and His plan to save them from themselves. Isaiah relays God's plan and promise of salvation, saying they will be so full of joy when this happens that the mountains will sing and the trees will clap their hands (Isa. 55:12).

When you read about the joy that God feels for His children, how does that affect your view of Him? Can you remember a time when you felt God's personal delight over you? Describe what it might feel like to know He's singing songs of joy about you.

Read Isaiah 55. What does this tell you about the relationship between following God and finding joy?

In his New Testament letters, the apostle Paul repeatedly encourages followers of Jesus to pursue joy as part of their relationship with God. He urges us to make rejoicing integral to how we live out our faith. And right after Paul's reminder to rejoice in the Lord at all times (Phil. 4:4), he gives specific instructions on how to do that: "Finally, brothers and sisters, whatever is true, whatever is noble, whatever is right, whatever is pure, whatever is lovely, whatever is admirable—if anything is excellent or praiseworthy—think about such things" (Phil. 4:8 NIV).

Life is complicated and sometimes difficult, and as devoted followers of God, we certainly do have many serious things to think about. We have hard things to ponder, sad situations that concern us, injustices that cause our hearts pain. But that's not all God wants for us. He also wants us to think about the lovely things of this world and the joy of our salvation yet to come. What a relief to know that we aren't required to leave laughter for the foolish and spend our days grim and gloomy. Instead, God invites us into a sacred space of big grins and loud laughs, of deep delight and light hearts.

God invites us into a sacred space of big grins and loud laughs, of deep delight and light hearts.

Read Psalm 100 aloud. Let the words minister to your soul as you turn them into a prayer for how you want to live with courageous joy. Write your prayer here.

Being a woman of courageous joy doesn't mean ignoring the painful and hard parts of life. Rather, it means continually remembering that God Himself is with you and delights in you and that He invites you to share in His delight. Read Deuteronomy 30:9; 2 Samuel 22:20; and Psalm 1:1–2 for words of assurance. Where will you look for joy in the Lord and with the Lord this week?

Reflect on this prayer and make it your own today:

God, I am so glad You never give up on me. You continue sending me love letters in the form of Your Word and Your creation and the many things that bring me joy and delight! Thank You for being an example and showing me the way to joy. Help me find it and hold on to it, Lord. Amen.

joy in the bad times

And now, dear brothers and sisters, we want you to
know what will happen to the believers who have died
so you will not grieve like people who have no hope.
For since we believe that Jesus died and was raised to
life again, we also believe that when Jesus returns, God
will bring back with him the believers who have died.

1 Thessalonians 4:13–14

My childhood was pebbled in grief, losing Mama when I was just nine and my beloved grandmother a year later. Great losses like these cut deep, leaving behind a valley of sorrow. My little wounded heart bled for a long, long while, until one day when I wasn't paying attention, it scabbed over and began to heal. Kindly, time has softened the jagged invisible scar that forever tattooed my heart.

The first time I met Sarah, my internal void sensed a mother's love. My now-husband and I had been dating seriously enough that it was time for me to meet his parents, so one weekend we slipped away from college and made the drive home. I was welcomed not only with open arms but also with an open heart.

My first impression proved lasting, and after marriage I received the blessing of "in-loves" ("in-laws" is too legal and cold to describe our relationship). It wasn't that Sarah was perfect, but she loved fully, reached out without being pushy, and pointed me to Jesus. Her only flaws might've been spoiling her grandbabies and loving her childhood sweetheart too much.

Decades later we downplayed the first signs of Sarah's dementia. At first it was simple things that were easily dismissed. But soon enough it was undeniable—a shuffling gait, parroting words, and what for me was the greatest "tell": making mistakes in the kitchen.

The last two years of Sarah's life were excruciating. We watched our dear mother, wife, grandmother, and friend wither away in mind and body. Oh, how I missed our conversations or calling her to clarify a recipe—blessings I had taken for granted.

Sarah's was a long, sad goodbye, the kind that led us to understand death's mercy. Because of how she ordered her life, her funeral service was a beautiful celebration. We were able to rejoice because the Lord was near. His peace *was* our comfort.

How amazing that our greatest grief in life—losing the people we love—can be the believer's greatest joy! What solace to know that even if given a chance to return, our loved ones would stay put in the presence of Jesus.

What great hope it brings us to realize that love doesn't die; *people* do. And because God is love and in Him we have new life, *eternal* life, our mourning will one day lead to joy forever.

—ROBIN DANCE

Have you ever experienced joy unexpectedly during a time of grief? How did that make you feel?

Grief is often understood as a synonym for sadness. It's defined as a singular though substantial emotion, when in fact it is a complicated process that encompasses many responses and feelings. Even the five stages of grief as defined by Elisabeth Kübler-Ross—denial, anger, bargaining, depression, acceptance[1]—are largely misunderstood as a rigid linear process people inevitably follow from point A to point B.

In reality, grief is messier and much more difficult to grasp than that.

Many who have experienced great loss or tragedy have learned this lesson, walking through the complexities of grief without a map or guide. In recognizing that grief is a kaleidoscope of feelings, they are less surprised to feel anger, relief, or guilt alongside deep sadness. Joy in the presence of grief, however, seems to confound nearly everyone.

When we lose a loved one or go through an unexpected life change such as divorce, illness, or unemployment, doubt creeps in from every side. And if we happen to feel a drop of joy in the midst of our darkest seasons, we frequently recoil from our own feelings. We feel confusion and even disgust that any part of us could let go of sorrow long enough to smile. How could we be happy at a time like this?

Think of a time you faced loss or pain. Did you experience distinct linear stages of grief? If not, how did it feel to experience more than one emotion at a time, or to grapple with certain emotions more than once?

Read Psalm 30. In what ways does it resonate with your experience when the author says the Lord has "turned my mourning into joyful dancing" (v. 11)? How has God given you a foundation for joy even when your feelings shift and change?

Paul knew how complicated a life of faith could be, especially when dealing with loss. That's why he addressed this very thing in his first letter to the church in Thessalonica, a community of new believers. The Thessalonians were confused about what happened to their loved ones after death, and they didn't know quite how to feel when processing their losses.

Was it okay that they were incredibly sad? Should they celebrate their loved ones now getting to spend eternity with God? But what about when Jesus comes back? Would they miss out on His glorious return, or would they somehow be part of that?

Just like we sometimes question our own reactions and emotions, people in the early church did too. They believed that Jesus would be returning within their lifetime, so they worried that their deceased friends and family members had departed too soon and would never be reunited with them or with the Lord.

When Paul heard about their misunderstanding and anxiety, he wrote to reassure them.

Read 1 Thessalonians 4:13–15 in the New International Reader's Version (you can find it on a Bible app or at BibleGateway.com). How does this translation change or add to your understanding of Paul's message here?

_____

_____

_____

_____

In clearing up any misunderstandings about what would happen to those who have already died when Jesus returns, Paul also reminds us that, as believers in a resurrected Christ, we have hope more powerful than the grave. He reminds us that, while death is final for those who do not know Jesus, we have been given the promise of eternity with God through the death and resurrection of Jesus. Because we believe in Him, we know that death has no permanent hold over us; therefore, we must not mourn in the same way as those without such hope.

This isn't to say we should not feel sad when faced with loss. No, Paul is not admonishing the real and reasonable feelings we experience when a loved one dies. Instead, he is comforting believers in their time of sorrow, encouraging us to find peace in the knowledge that our pain is temporary and relief is coming.

Grief during a time of loss does not indicate a lack of faith, just as joy interspersed with harsher emotions does not indicate a lack of sorrow, compassion, or depth. As Robin wrote, joy does come in the mourning when we can rejoice in God's love, provision, and plans—even when we don't

> When our feelings seem confusing or fickle, the Lord is constant and faithful.

understand His plans and can't fully comprehend His love. And even when our feelings seem confusing or fickle, the Lord is constant and faithful.

Write out the second part of Psalm 30:5 in your own words. How does this truth affect how you live today?

_____

_____

_____

_____

_____

Finding joy while we're also grieving can be difficult for a number of reasons, including how others might perceive us. How does choosing joy in every circumstance require courage from you?

_____

_____

_____

_____

_____

Reflect on this prayer and make it your own today:

Lord, thank You for promising to be near to the brokenhearted. Thank You for every way You bring us joy, even during our darkest hours. Please be with me today and help me find my way to joyful dancing. Give me the courage to choose joy and the faith to trust You in every circumstance. Amen.

Through Jesus, therefore, let us continually offer to God a sacrifice of praise—the fruit of lips that openly profess his name.

Hebrews 13:15 NIV

I stood next to my husband in the second row of the worship room. The few inches between us felt more like a million-mile chasm. The praise band led us with fervor, but I could barely move my lips to the lyrics. Instead, my lips quivered and tears ran rivers down my face.

Everything had become too much—uprooting our family to move back to our hometown, the loneliness in our marriage, our toddler waking up screaming every couple hours in the middle of the night. The weight of it all dragged me over the edge of sanity, and there at the bottom of the pit, depression threatened to unravel my mind and my faith.

How can I sing these songs? How can I clap and celebrate God's goodness or His power when I can barely make it through the day?

It seemed false to sing words that rang hollow in my life at the moment. I wasn't convinced that forcing the lyrics and notes to come out of my throat would be offering true worship to God, so I didn't sing. I stood there, arms limp at my sides, letting the voices of others carry me into the presence of God.

I came to Him that day with nothing but my tears, nothing but broken things in my hands, nothing but confusion and pain and doubt, nothing but silence. But there was no condemnation from Him, no stern look of disapproval at my lack of singing or anything resembling what we consider as worship. Instead, it was His gentleness that met me and reminded me that Christ did it all already. His death on the cross was the ultimate offering of worship to God, and through Him, the little I bring to the altar is made into a pleasing fragrance to God.

I may not have been singing the songs, but God received my quivering lips and my desperate cries that still professed His nearness—and therefore, His goodness—to me.

—GRACE P. CHO

Have you ever had a hard time worshiping during a difficult or painful season? What happened when you were finally able to surrender and sacrifice your praise and your pain to God?

When we're most distraught or desperate, sometimes the only thing that seems certain is our pain. And so, despite knowing it's not good for us, we hold tightly to the thing that is hurting us so deeply. We hold the line, we hold grudges, we hold on to our rights—all in an attempt to control the pain.

Instead of holding on to everything that hurts us, we must cling to the Lord and let go of the rest.

What we don't realize (or what we forget) is that God is right there with us, offering to carry our burden. All we have to do is release our hold on it. We must let go of our illusions of control, trusting God and praising Him for His provision and His plan. Instead of holding on to everything that hurts us, we must cling to the Lord and let go of the rest. He's asking us to acknowledge that only He can control the wind and the world and the things that hurt us, that only He can comfort us and heal us. He's asking us to give a sacrifice of praise.

> Psalm 94:19 says, "When anxiety was great within me, your consolation brought me joy" (NIV). Reflect on a time when the Lord eased your fear or pain and brought you joy.

> What is standing in the way of your fully trusting God? How might that be keeping you from offering your praise to Him?

This struggle is something Paul was familiar with. He told the church in Corinth that God gave him a persistent physical ailment to keep him humble, and though his prayers for healing seemed to go unanswered, he thanked and praised God that His grace was sufficient (2 Cor. 12:5–10). When we read Romans 5:3–5, we can see that Paul recommends facing trials with rejoicing because they will help us grow in faith and character.

Paul knew that his trust was not misplaced and that his hope would not lead to disappointment. Instead, he had faith that God would be glorified in his weakness and that his pain would not be wasted. He knew—and even boasted—that apart from God he had nothing to offer anyone; likewise, he knew that he had nothing to offer God except his love, obedience, and praise. That is how Paul was able to let go of any perceived control he had over his situation and offer his open hands and heart to God.

Paul's commitment to rejoicing during trials didn't waver, even when he was beaten and imprisoned. Though most of us won't go through such extreme persecution, we can be inspired to hold fast to our faith and find joy when we face disappointments and challenges such as job loss, infertility, divorce, loneliness, or the death of a loved one.

Read Acts 16:16–34. What did Paul and Silas do when they were treated so horribly? What did God do in response? How do you think Paul and Silas found the strength to sing praises to God in the middle of this experience, even before they saw God's provision or plan?

Think of a painful or difficult situation you are currently facing or have experienced in the past. What can you praise God for right now, even if He has not removed the "thorn" in your flesh or solved your problem?

_____

_____

_____

Just as Grace surrendered her pain to God during worship in her church and Paul and Silas sang hymns in prison, we can rejoice and praise God during our hardest times because we can trust that He is with us. We can lean on the truth that He is a good and loving God (1 John 4:9–10) and that He will work all things for our good (Rom. 8:28). Like the old hymn says, no matter what storms we face, God teaches us to proclaim, "It is well with my soul."

Praising God when life is difficult *is* a sacrifice. It takes strength, faith, and courage to stop fixating on our pain and circumstances and start focusing on God. How can you surrender your hard situations into God's hands? How will you offer a sacrifice of praise today?

_____

_____

_____

_____

Reflect on this prayer and make it your own today:

God, it feels impossible to whisper a word of praise right now, much less sing a song of rejoicing. Will You help me? Open my eyes to the many blessings I still hold and all the reasons You've given me to rejoice. Open my hands as I surrender control, and open my heart and my lips to give You the praise You deserve. Thank You, God. Amen.

Rejoice in the LORD always. I will say it again: Rejoice!
Let your graciousness be known to everyone. The LORD
is near. Don't worry about anything, but in everything,
through prayer and petition with thanksgiving, present
your requests to God. And the peace of God, which
surpasses all understanding, will guard your hearts and
minds in Christ Jesus.

Philippians 4:4–7 CSB

A couple weeks ago we invited a friend over for dinner. It was the first time we'd had him over, and as he walked into our living room and glanced around our home, he said, "Your house isn't *that* small!"

He'd heard me complain about it for years. And while I was certain his visit would confirm every bad thing I'd ever said about our falling-apart, impossible-to-sell tiny old house, it seemed to do the opposite. Our friend walked around our dining room, asking my husband about the "interesting" textured walls and peering down the hallway as if it led to an east wing instead of three small bedrooms and an even smaller bathroom.

After he left, I thought about how distorted my perspective had gotten after living in our "starter" home for nearly thirteen years.

During bedtime prayers with my daughter each night, I try to force gratitude on myself by thanking God for a house to live in. And I know full well that millions of people live in much worse conditions that I can't even fathom. A fridge that leaks or floors that squeak are absolutely not the end of the world, and the fact that my two daughters have their own bedrooms and our garage is full of all the stuff *that won't fit in our house* makes us fortunate, if not spoiled.

Yet when I'm honest with myself, I must admit that most often I feel resentment toward my home. You know, that lovely combination of disappointment, bitterness, and envy? Yeah, that.

I don't want to feel that way—or act that way or teach my kids to be that way. I want to be satisfied with what I have and thankful for all I've been given. Regardless of what the world says I need to be happy (newer! bigger! fancier!), I know the Lord calls us to be thankful at all times, to choose joy no matter what our surroundings or circumstances look like.

It's not easy, but I get to choose whether I face the challenges, the frustrations, the disappointments of life with a joyful heart or a bitter one. Choosing joy requires a strength I don't have, a reserve I can only find when I lean on God and allow Him to turn my resentment to rejoicing.

—MARY CARVER

In what ways have you gotten caught up in what the world values or deems worthy of praise and gratitude?

_____

_____

_____

_____

_____

Have you ever noticed that some of the most cheerful, joyful people are those who suffer the most (at least by the world's standards)? How is this possible? Don't they know how bad they have it? Or is it possible they actually know something sacred about joy and suffering?

Sara Frankl lived with a rare, terminal autoimmune disease that caused her chronic, horrific pain. After years of complications and medications, Sara eventually became housebound, literally allergic to the outside world. Though she once dreamed of having a husband and kids, she had to let go of those dreams—as well as her career as a writer, her love of singing in church and at weddings, and the active social and family life she adored—and surrender to isolation as her disease ran its course.

Sara died at age thirty-eight, but during her darkest, most painful days she drew incredible strength from her faith. She made the phrase "choose joy" her personal mantra, embodying Peter's words to persecuted Christians: "Instead, rejoice as you share in the sufferings of Christ, so that you may also rejoice with great joy when his glory is revealed" (1 Pet. 4:13 CSB). Sara wrote, "I choose the joy. When something is going badly and I'm dwelling on it, I think instead of something for which I am grateful. I swear to you, it's as simple as that. You just have to decide today, and again tomorrow. And before you know it, you'll have an attitude of joy more than any other attitude you have at your disposal."[2]

Do you think choosing joy is simple? What makes it feel like a simple or complicated choice?

_____

_____

_____

_____

What is one way your life looks different from what the world says is required for a person to be happy? Where do you see God working in that situation?

Though Sara spoke honestly when she said her decision to choose joy was simple, she never claimed it was easy. She wrote openly about her pain, which then allowed her to illustrate all the more clearly the supernatural work God can do when we surrender to Him and rejoice in Him no matter what.

We see this breathtaking acceptance and trust in God when we read the story of Joseph in the Old Testament. Ambushed by his jealous brothers and sold into slavery, then later falsely accused and imprisoned, Joseph suffered greatly through no fault of his own. But rather than becoming bitter and resentful, Joseph chose to trust God's sovereignty.

Years later, a famine brought Joseph and his brothers back together. Read Genesis 50:15–21. Based on what he said to his brothers, how did Joseph view the difficult road that had brought him to his position as second-in-command over Egypt?

----

week 5 • day 3

Read Jeremiah 29:10–14. What do these promises from God—originally given to the Israelites living in exile—say about our own difficult circumstances?

Accepting less-than-ideal circumstances can feel impossible, and when you compare your life with someone else's, it can be tempting to play the "It's not fair!" card. But we can learn an important lesson from Joseph and Jeremiah (and from Sara Frankl). We can listen to God when He says He loves us and has a plan for us. We can choose to rejoice rather than resent, and to value spiritual blessings and maturity more than earthly riches or physical comfort. When the world tempts us to wish for more, better, newer, and shinier, we can ask God to open our eyes to what He's doing in our lives right now, right where we are.

> When the world tempts us to wish for more, better, newer, and shinier, we can ask God to open our eyes to what He's doing in our lives right now, right where we are.

The world might look at your situation and insist it's impossible to find joy in it, but God promises you can. How can you turn from resenting your reality to courageously rejoicing today?

Reflect on this prayer and make it your own today:

Dear Lord, life feels really hard right now. If I compare my life to what the world tells me matters most, I come up short and end up resentful. Please forgive me for feeling bitter. Please show me how to find joy, even in this, and how to trust You and Your good plans for me. Amen.

Truly I tell you, you will weep and mourn, but the world will rejoice. You will become sorrowful, but your sorrow will turn to joy. When a woman is in labor, she has pain because her time has come. But when she has given birth to a child, she no longer remembers the suffering because of the joy that a person has been born into the world. So you also have sorrow now. But I will see you again. Your hearts will rejoice, and no one will take away your joy from you.

John 16:20–22 CSB

Once upon a time, in a not-so-distant past, my family moved twice in the same year. First we moved in with my mom, then we moved into our new home.

You know that old saying "When it rains, it pours"? In addition to moving, we were under a deluge. From August until November, most of our belongings were packed into a storage unit. In September I self-published my first book, packing up and mailing out orders from my mom's living room. By October we'd made offers on six houses, and each had been turned down. In November my youngest child turned one, and we finally moved into our new home (the seventh offer) just before Thanksgiving. My sister got married on New Year's Eve, and as the matron of honor I hosted her bridal shower and bachelorette brunch and got my family ready to be the ring bearer, flower girls, and a groomsman. In December my oldest child turned five and we celebrated his birthday, Christmas, and my sister's wedding.

It was a season we'll never forget, and it came to mind recently as I made oatmeal. I remembered making the same hearty breakfast as we prepared to move. We were half packed at that point, so many of our kitchen items were in boxes. I hadn't been doing much cooking because of the inconvenience, but this day in our still-half-ours home, I pulled out my trusty old slow cooker for overnight oats.

I chopped and measured, poured and stirred. I ruffled little heads that ran by and I stooped to hand over a refilled sippy cup. As I prepared the simplest of meals in my messy kitchen, I felt peace replace stress in my heart, my shoulders, my brain.

My frayed nerves were soothed, I was calmer, and I breathed deeper. I was kinder to my family. I was motivated. I went to bed early, and I was satisfied with how the day had gone.

That day in my half-packed, running-out-of-groceries, crumb-covered kitchen, God gave me a stream. A cool, refreshing oasis in a parched land of daily tasks that had dried out my soul. He used twenty minutes of simple meal preparation to create a pool in the burning sand of my heart.

Our God makes much of our small offerings.

A few minutes of kitchen prep can fill us up. The chapel of our heart can become His cathedral. God's love leaves a lingering calm that can reign in us when we feel anything but peaceful.

—ANNA RENDELL

Think back to a time of chaos and confusion in your life. What regular routine or habit were you able to maintain or restart? How did those "normal" tasks in the midst of unusual circumstances affect your heart and mind?

Chaos comes in all shapes and colors. Sometimes it appears when life is overwhelmingly busy; other times it's a result of sadness or grief. Regardless of where it starts, that chaos can make it hard to handle the everyday tasks that keep our lives and our minds calm. We can be tempted to give in to the disorder and allow ourselves to be blown about by emotions and circumstances. But God never leaves us alone in our suffering.

He promises to be with the brokenhearted (Ps. 34:18), and He promises to extend His hand and give us a way out.

Read 1 Corinthians 10:13. How have you been tempted when going through a time of grief or suffering? How do you resist spinning out of control inside when your world is falling apart (or even when you are simply trudging through the mundane days of life)?

As the time for Jesus's death came near, He knew the disciples would experience a flood of emotions. Just as Paul promised the Corinthians that God would provide a way out of temptation, Jesus promised relief for the disciples' grief. In fact, He told them they'd be rejoicing soon. "So you also have sorrow now. But I will see you again. Your hearts will rejoice, and no one will take away your joy from you" (John 16:22 CSB).

Can you imagine? As crowds shouted for Jesus's crucifixion, the disciples reeled in shock and grief. Talk about a world falling apart! They must have felt such confusion, as their expectations of who the Messiah would be crumbled and events they never could have imagined took place right before their eyes. In that moment they couldn't comprehend the coming resurrection and the joy it would bring.

In the confusing days following Jesus's resurrection, the disciples went fishing. It's what they knew. It's where they came from. Maybe they hoped to gain clarity about what had happened or find answers to their remaining questions. It wouldn't solve all their problems or make their future clear, but it was something.

So they grabbed their nets and headed out. But they didn't catch a thing . . . until the next morning when Jesus appeared and told them to cast their nets on the other side of the boat (John 21:1–6).

Instead of just sitting and being swallowed by their unusual situation, the disciples did the next thing—and that is exactly where Jesus found them. He showed up in the middle of their everyday task, comforting them and bringing them more fish than they could count and more hope than they could measure.

Read the entire story of when the disciples went fishing and encountered the risen Christ in John 21:1–14. How do you think the other disciples felt when Simon Peter said, "I am going fishing"? How would you feel in that situation?

How do your daily tasks or habits help you find joy in the Lord? Some examples could be expressing gratitude for God's provision when putting away groceries or washing dishes, or asking for God's protection over your family as you fold laundry.

_____

_____

_____

_____

_____

Nowhere in God's Word does He demand that we should be unaffected by the world around us. Jesus says outright that we'll have "many trials and sorrows" (John 16:33). But as followers of Christ who put our hope in Him, we don't have to be consumed by the difficulties we face. Even when we're experiencing stress and anxiety, hardship and trial, we can pause, turn to the Lord as we do the next simple thing, and find peace once again.

> **Even when we're experiencing stress and anxiety, hardship and trial, we can pause, turn to the Lord as we do the next simple thing, and find peace once again.**

Look up John 16:22 in several translations. (Use BibleGateway.com, where you can compare the same verse in different translations, or use a Bible app.) Now write it in your own words, perhaps as if Jesus were speaking directly to you. What is He saying?

_____

_____

What is one thing you can do today to bring your focus back to the Lord and His provision for you? Think small and immediate; don't get distracted right now by the long-term. How might this increase your courage and trust in His plans for you in this life?

Reflect on this prayer and make it your own today:

God, thank You for the ordinary, regular, mundane tasks You give us. Thank You for a way out of temptation and turmoil, a pathway from panic to peace. Keep my eyes focused on You while my hands work on the things You've put in front of me. Please help me find joy in the small things. Amen.

Do not grieve, because the joy of the LORD is your strength.

Nehemiah 8:10 CSB

I rocked my toddler and prayed the warm misty air would soothe his lungs and offer some relief. Croup always seems to hit in the middle of the night, stealing my peacefully sleeping babe and replacing him with a barking imposter.

Jude fussed and fidgeted on my lap. He played with my hairbrush until he chucked it on the floor in protest of being sick and tired. My eyelids begged to close, but my boy needed a few more minutes of steamy therapy. So I began to sing. My usual soothing bedtime melodies came out on autopilot. "Jesus Loves Me," then "Gentle Shepherd" and "As the Deer."

Then, without a conscious thought or decision, I found the words of "Silent Night" pouring from my lips. *Silent night. Holy night. All is calm. All is bright.*

I rubbed Jude's back. His little body snuggled into mine and his breathing settled.

It was barely October and Christmas was hardly on my radar. But there in my steam-filled bathroom, with dingy grout and a pile of the kids' discarded clothes crumpled on the floor, the words of this classic Christmas carol washed over my heart.

I imagined how the air in that stable where the Christ child was born might have also been thick and steamy from the sweat of labor, the hot breath of animals, and the stench of manure. I thought about how this sweet melodic song was really depicting a story that could not have been nearly as picturesque as our Christmas cards and nativity figurines might lead us to believe.

Yet after the chaos and struggle of labor, there was a child. A holy child whose presence must have eased His mother's pain and made a smelly stable holy. Heaven's peace filled that otherwise ordinary space.

In the middle of the night, in the middle of my worry, God met me through the words of a Christmas carol. And He whispered to my weary heart, *I love you. I am here, filling THIS musty, ordinary room. My heavenly peace is available to you too. I am holy. Praise Me for My holiness!*

I didn't want to be pulled from the comfort of my warm bed to care for a sick child, but what a gift it turned out to be. Because there in my steamy bathroom, Jesus was present and my heart was filled with joy. Not happiness for the circumstances, but true joy in Christ.

—BECKY KEIFE

When has God met you in an unexpected place—perhaps somewhere (or in some situation) you did not want to be? What did it feel like to realize He was with you?

Sometimes we find ourselves abundantly blessed when we were expecting the opposite. We feel irritated to share an armrest on a long flight, but we end up having the most encouraging conversation with a stranger. We resent getting out of bed to soothe a child, but the hugs of unconditional love soften our rough edges. We feel too busy for the coffee date or the volunteer hours we committed to, but the relationships we nurture end up being heart-nourishing or even life-changing.

In the book of Nehemiah, we see the transformation the Israelites went through after the walls of Jerusalem were rebuilt. At this time the people of God were just as broken as their city walls had been, and it was time to address that. The leaders gathered all the people to listen to Ezra, the priest and scribe, read the law of God.

The people were quickly overwhelmed with grief as they faced the great gap between God's law and their actions and hearts. But Nehemiah and Ezra would not allow them to stay stuck in that sorrow. They reminded the people that it was a holy day and urged them instead to rejoice in God's love.

Like the Israelites, we are incapable of closing the gap between our heart and God's without His great love and mercy. And without His strength freely offered to us (Isa. 41:10), we can't get past our grief once our eyes are opened. We need an Ezra and a Nehemiah to remind us of the joy we can find with God's strength, which leads us to rest securely in His love and "rejoice greatly" (Neh. 8:12 NKJV).

Read the following verses, often called "the Romans Road to Salvation." They explain with clarity and urgency how our sin separates us from God and how we can be reconciled to Him. Our response to these verses may be similar to that of the Israelites when they heard Ezra read the law and speak about God's love. Record your observations and anything God speaks to you about these things.

Romans 3:10

Romans 3:23

Romans 5:8

Romans 6:23

Romans 10:9–10

Romans 10:13

_____

_____

_____

_____

_____

Have you ever felt overwhelmed with sadness about either your own sin or the reality of living in a world full of sin? As you consider these things, read John 3:17. How do these words of Jesus comfort you and even bring you joy?

_____

_____

_____

_____

When Paul wrote his letter to the Romans, he made a solid case for why we need Jesus. He laid it out clearly, as you can see from the verses we just read. We all have sinned. Therefore, we cannot be in relationship with God. But God loves us so much, He's given us a way to be saved from our sin and reunited with Him.

As we talked about on day 2 earlier this week, Paul says that we should rejoice in our afflictions because they produce faith and character and hope. That instruction seems impossible to follow until we remember this: the joy of the Lord is our strength. When we're weary under the weight of our sorrows, we don't have to carry them alone. When we're brokenhearted and bleeding from the wounds of this world, we don't stay in that sadness alone.

God is with us (Ps. 34:18) and offers to carry our burdens, to point us back to the hope and peace we find only in Him. And that is worth rejoicing about!

> When we're weary under the weight of our sorrows, we don't have to carry them alone. The joy of the Lord is our strength.

Imagine you are holding your burdens in your hands right now. The burdens you created yourself and the ones the world foisted onto you. The ones you think you can handle and the ones that threaten to push you under this very minute. Every disappointment, every worry, every illness, every challenge—hold them in your hands.

Now read the invitation Jesus offers in Matthew 11:28–30. What would it take to let go of every single burden and to turn them over to God? How can you courageously choose to receive all the comfort, strength, and joy the Lord has for you today?

When we are reminded of our sinful nature, when we are awakened in the middle of the night by a sick toddler or a curfew-breaking teenager, when a flat tire or a phone call with news we never expected derails our plans for the day—or for life—we can still choose to rejoice. Not because our challenges and griefs are magically erased, but because we know someday they will be. In the meantime, God is still working.

Do you need to fall into the arms of your Father today? What is causing you pain? Where do you most need strength and endurance?

Keeping a gratitude list or joy journal is one way to strengthen our faith and trust in the Lord. List three ways God has met you during a difficult time or ways you have found joy even when life is hard.

Reflect on this prayer and make it your own today:

Dear God, thank You for loving me even while I am a sinner. Please forgive me for the ways I've fallen short, and keep me close to You. Thank You for being with me and for giving me Your strength when life gets too heavy and too hard. Thank You for offering joy in every circumstance, even the hardest ones. You are my joy. Amen.

joy in community

I appeal to you, dear brothers and sisters, by the authority of our LORD Jesus Christ, to live in harmony with each other. Let there be no divisions in the church. Rather, be of one mind, united in thought and purpose.

1 Corinthians 1:10

It felt like just another normal day. I was feeding my kids and doing some laundry when my Voxer app began exploding with messages. One of my friends had just been spit on; another was in tears after being taunted on the sidewalk with shouts of "Coronavirus!" I pulled up Facebook and saw that while another friend had been sitting on his front porch, someone driving by shouted racial slurs at him simply because he's Korean.

These are just a few examples of racism against Asian American people—people like me. They were the most recent in a long line of my own experiences and encounters I had witnessed in the past week, and I was exhausted—mentally, emotionally, and physically. A visceral reaction kicks in every time I personally experience racism or witness it on social media and with my friends. It's that mix of anger and pain when hot tears stream down my face and it becomes hard to breathe. It's overwhelming, and it happens every time.

Minorities like me are entrenched in the fight against racism. It's part of our daily reality to both survive and thrive. Labels are forced on us, whether we like it or not, because of the color of our skin. And the thing is, it's easy to become angry, bitter, and disillusioned at the world.

But it's at that very moment that I need to pause and pray. I know myself. I'm quick to point out racism, and in the following days I would begin pursuing actionable responses. Because racism cannot be confronted unless justice is demanded. But I also need to make sure my radar is just as sensitive to the ways in which God sovereignly and graciously preserves the lives of people of color. My thoughts don't naturally gravitate in that direction, but I need this reminder to know that all hope is not lost and that I am not alone.

After praying for God to bring His justice and end the evils of racism, I spent time in praise for the work God is doing in our churches and ministries, spaces that are no longer white-centered but Christ-centered, and that honor the lives and dignity of all peoples. Though this world is full of evil, God is always good! And He has also raised up allies to expose and oppose systemic oppression against minorities. Reminding myself of these truths in the face of racism helps me to still find joy and take things one step at a time. I'm not alone. God is sovereign, and His justice is coming. And for now, I can take another breath and rest in that.

—MICHELLE REYES

Think of a time when you witnessed division and injustice in your community. How did that make you feel toward others? Did it cause you to think of God any differently?

When the apostle Paul wrote to the believers in Corinth, he addressed division in their church community. He begins the first chapter of 1 Corinthians by saying, "I appeal to you, dear brothers and sisters, by the authority of our Lord Jesus Christ, to live in harmony with each other. Let there be no divisions in the church. Rather, be of one mind, united in thought and purpose" (1:10). Later in the book we get a fuller picture of a specific conflict.

In chapter 11 Paul writes about the way the church was observing the Lord's Supper (or what many now call communion). He reminds them of its true purpose: to remember the sacrifice Jesus made for us (vv. 23–26). But the bigger issue he addresses involves the meals that typically took place alongside the Lord's Supper. Instead of sharing food and drink with everyone in the church, the wealthy feasted while the poor went hungry. This was typical behavior in ancient Roman culture, but Paul makes it clear that such discrimination and selfishness are unacceptable for believers in Christ (1 Cor. 11:20–22).

Who is being neglected in your community? Read Jeremiah 22:3 and Micah 6:8. What would it look like to implement these instructions in your community? How would God be glorified through these changes?

How important is it to Jesus that we get along? (Hint: read His words
recorded in Matt. 5:9, 43–48; 7:12; and 25:40.)

_____

_____

_____

_____

_____

Paul doesn't stop at pointing out exactly why the divisive practices of the Lord's Supper were harmful and what the Corinthians should do instead. In chapter 12 he goes on to explain how their differences could be used in a way that would benefit them and their community, as well as honor God. He begins by acknowledging that the body of believers is diverse but that everyone serves the same God.

Read 1 Corinthians 12:4–19. Paul points out that each person in the church is created uniquely and that they all fit together perfectly as one body—the body of Christ. A human body is created so that certain parts protect weaker or smaller parts, and the body of Christ is designed in much the same way. In addition, as interlocked and interdependent parts of one body, when one person or group is hurting, all the others feel pain too.

When the body isn't working together and each individual part is going its own way—or worse, belittling, overlooking, or competing against other parts of the body—the result is turmoil, strife, and a lack of peace. Joy is not possible unless we do the good, hard work of valuing every believer.

Joy is not possible unless we do the good, hard work of valuing every believer.

Can you imagine the pain God must feel when He sees His kids fighting and dividing? Conversely, what incredible joy He must experience when all the parts of His body are connecting and benefiting one another as He intended. That's the joy we get to share when we overcome harmful patterns in our communities and churches with the courage that comes from Christ.

Everything Paul told the early church in Corinth is true for today's church. We have been created beautifully diverse with the goal of fitting together in the most intricate way to honor and serve and glorify our Creator. If we treat our brothers and sisters badly—especially if we do so *because* of our differences—we are not only hurting them but hurting ourselves and the Lord. Just like the Corinthians, we must do better. We must truly love God and love others by embracing and celebrating what makes us unique. Only then can we enjoy the gift of being one.

> ## We must truly love God and love others by embracing and celebrating what makes us unique.

Read John 17:20–23. What was Jesus's prayer for future believers? What did He say living this out would communicate to the rest of the world?

_____

_____

_____

_____

_____

Loving our neighbors, pursuing unity, living in harmony—even when we wholeheartedly agree with these goals, they can be difficult to live out in our everyday. Fortunately, the Bible is full of wisdom that's directly applicable.

Look up at least three of the following passages (but feel free to read all of them):

Psalm 82:3   Proverbs 31:8–9

Proverbs 10:12   Ephesians 4:31–32

Proverbs 14:31   Colossians 3:12–14

Proverbs 15:18   1 John 3:17–18

Which of these verses resonates most strongly with you? What is God telling you today about what He wants for you and your relationships with other believers?

Read Romans 15:1–13. Paul urges us to live in harmony, both for the good of the church as a whole and for our own joy in how God designed us as individuals. What specific step will you take this week to begin finding and sharing more joy in your community, particularly with people who are different from you?

Reflect on this prayer and make it your own today:

God, I'm so humbled to realize that Jesus prayed for our unity two thousand years ago. I'm also relieved to know I'm not the first person to struggle with this, and I'm grateful You provide the pathway to becoming a family who loves one another the way You love us. Please forgive me for the times I've treated others badly, judged them because of our differences, and served myself before considering their needs. Open my eyes, Lord, and help me love my brothers and sisters as You do. Amen.

Let us think of ways to motivate one another to acts of love and good works. And let us not neglect our meeting together, as some people do, but encourage one another.

Hebrews 10:24-25

L ast year I watched *Yesterday*, a movie about Jack, a musician who finally made it big after years of struggling.

One scene shows Jack performing his biggest concert ever at a hometown venue that had once canceled a small gig he played because no one showed up except his trio of friends. Not even his parents believed in him! But those friends who had supported him all along— showing up at every sparsely attended performance he booked, cheering wholeheartedly for every set, requesting his signature song just one more time—were standing front and center at that huge concert. They yelled and waved signs asking him to play that song, the one he'd written before anyone else knew his name, before he'd experienced an ounce of success.

This picture of friendship moved me deeply, bringing to mind those who have stood by me despite my own failing and floundering as I've pursued my dreams. I was reminded of how much I appreciate the people who have supported me in all my ventures, of how grateful I am that they've walked with me and shown up for me and encouraged me whenever I've felt frustrated or disappointed. And I thought of the times I've been overwhelmed with joy and excitement for them, grateful for the opportunity to celebrate a friend's success or good news.

Jesus well knew the importance of supporting and celebrating one another. Though it seems incredible to us now, Jesus's family did not believe (at first) that He was the Messiah. They thought He was crazy (Mark 3:20–21), and the people of His hometown weren't much better, scoffing and becoming offended at His actions and words (Mark 6:1–6).

But Jesus didn't waste time or energy chasing the approval of those who ignored or criticized Him. He didn't neglect the ones who truly supported Him—the ones who weren't family but became family—in favor of pursuing the ones He *thought* should be on His team. Nope. He recognized who was there day after day, and He poured into those men and women. He loved them well, served them, and served alongside them.

We should do the same—locking arms with those beside us, being filled with gratitude for their support and for the chance to support them in return. Let's champion and love one another with encouraging words and with our presence. Let's show up and listen hard and stand in the very front row, waving our banners and cheering each other on.

—MARY CARVER

What does it look like in your life to show up for a friend? When have you received the sweet gift of celebration and support from friends or family? How did that make you feel?

When you think of the apostle Paul, what comes to mind? Is it his dramatic conversion to Christianity (Acts 9:1–19)? His great success as a church planter and preacher? Perhaps you think of his New Testament letters—the ones that seem to come from a stern older brother. Or maybe you recall the man with a thorn in his flesh who talks about being joyful in all circumstances.

But have you ever thought about the incredible joy he found in his friends and fellow followers of Jesus? Read the following verses from Paul's letters to the churches in Philippi and Thessalonica:

Philippians 1:3–6

1 Thessalonians 2:17–20

1 Thessalonians 3:9–10

Paul couldn't keep from expressing affection for his friends. Even in jail, he found joy in his community!

The above passages were written to believers at churches Paul helped start. What do his words tell you about his friendships and the value he placed on them? What does that tell you about what God wants for your own friendships?

Think about a time when you supported or encouraged a friend who was struggling. How did coming alongside someone else increase your own joy?

_____

_____

_____

_____

When Paul writes in Romans 12:15 that we should "rejoice with those who rejoice" and "weep with those who weep" (CSB), he isn't simply passing on another rule for Christian living. He is sharing sound wisdom. When we share one another's burdens and sorrows, we lighten their load. But when we rejoice with one another, our joy is multiplied.

So why not share your joy with others?

Why do you think God wants us to celebrate (rejoice) with one another? Why does it matter to Him if our happiness is increased?

_____

_____

_____

_____

It's true that celebrating the big and small wins is so much more enjoyable when we do so together, but not simply because it makes us feel happier. Sharing in someone else's joy as if it were our own also strengthens the body of Christ.

One of the reasons Paul expressed such great joy in the believers he wrote to is that they were following God. Knowing that they had trusted Jesus for their salvation and that they were living out their faith in tangible ways made him exceptionally happy. Because he loved the believers so much, he wanted to encourage them to continue living according to God's plan—and then he urged them to also support one another. He concluded his letter to the church at Corinth this way: "Dear brothers and sisters, I close my letter with these last words: Be joyful. Grow to maturity. Encourage each other. Live in harmony and peace. Then the God of love and peace will be with you" (2 Cor. 13:11).

> Sharing in someone else's joy as if it were your own also strengthens the body of Christ.

Encouraging each other—supporting one another when times are hard, celebrating together when times are wonderful, weeping with those who weep, rejoicing with those who rejoice—is not just a suggestion. It was an integral part of Paul's life and testimony, and it's a critical part of our lives as believers today.

This encouragement might look like praying for a friend before a job interview, sending balloons to celebrate a new baby or a completed project, holding a friend's hand in a hospital waiting room, volunteering to support a friend's ministry, or sending a thank-you card to someone who has influenced your own faith. Any way you show kindness and compassion to other people will be a testimony to God's love lived out by His followers. And that's something to celebrate!

Near the end of 1 Thessalonians, Paul once again reminds us to encourage one another. Look up 1 Thessalonians 5:11. Compare different translations (you can do this easily at BibleGateway.com or with a Bible app) and write down the one that resonates most with you.

_____

_____

Who can you cheer on this week? Think about your friends and family, the people you go to church with, or perhaps your coworkers. Who can you celebrate for doing a good job, for being a good friend, or simply for being themselves? Take a note from Paul and courage from the Lord and tell that person how much they mean to you.

Reflect on this prayer and make it your own today:

God, I'm so thankful for the people You've placed in my life. Help me to champion and encourage my friends and family this week. I want them to know how much joy they give me, but more importantly, how much joy I find in You. Please show me opportunities to support others in their faith and genuinely share in their joy. Help me love You and love others well. Amen.

Make a joyful noise to the LORD, all the earth!
  Serve the LORD with gladness!
  Come into his presence with singing!
                        Psalm 100:1–2 ESV

I know the psalmist says to make a joyful noise unto the Lord, but when the soloist sang, I heard zero joy and all noise! I likened his voice to the sound of cat claws clashing with a chalkboard. How was I supposed to focus on God when I was using all of my energy to block out the soloist's awful voice? And who thought it was a good idea to let him lead the worship music?

I was furious with my pastor! He'd prompted our Bible study group to gather for worship with this ministry group whose music set was culturally different from ours. You see, our traditionally Black church was in the process of transitioning into a multiethnic church. So our pastor was constantly guiding us across traditional lines of division.

Initially, music style inclusion was painful. I simply wanted the comfort of the Black gospel sound that I believed was God's true soundtrack. And I wanted the deep, complex harmonies of the Black gospel choirs of John P. Kee and Kirk Franklin to usher me *into His gates with thanksgiving and into His courts with praise*. In my mind's ear, Vineyard and Hillsong did not measure up, and this soloist's rendition furthered the dissonance.

In the midst of all the noise—the culturally different music, the pitch-challenged vocalist, and my complaining—I had to make the choice to reach for the truth of my identity. "God is spirit, and His worshipers must worship in the Spirit and in truth" (John 4:24 NIV). I am His worshiper; that's who I am. So I stopped obsessing over my discomfort and leaned into the spirit and truth of what was happening.

Culturally and racially different followers of Jesus, who typically worshiped separately, gathered as one in this moment to gaze on God's goodness. We had abandoned our personal preferences and left our comfort zones in solidarity with God's dream. And when I shifted my focus from what I wanted to what God was doing, my spirit broke free from the confines of my preferences. The noise faded and I was able to hear the purest intention of the soloist's offering of worship. And I found my joy again.

—LUCRETIA BERRY

How do you redirect your focus to God when you feel distracted during a worship service because the music, the message style, or the order of service is not what you are used to or prefer?

_____

_____

_____

_____

"Have it your way" was a revolutionary ad slogan in the fast-food restaurant industry. When Burger King began using that catchphrase in 1974 to tell customers they could order their sandwiches with any combination of condiments and toppings they wanted, it was a novel business model. Today, however, we can have it our way at most restaurants—and it doesn't stop there. We can order shampoo or skin-care products created for our individual needs. We can cut cable and subscribe to just the channels and streaming services that play our favorite shows. We can follow and unfollow people and businesses until our social media feeds give us only the updates we agree with or appreciate. And we can subscribe to any number of gift boxes that send us carefully curated items designed to please us personally.

None of this is inherently bad. But the fact remains that we live in a highly customizable society—and if we're not careful, our perspective can narrow while our sense of entitlement grows. All of that, then, can trickle into the way we seek God, how we worship Him, and how we live in fellowship with other believers.

Given the number of churches in most cities and the number of teaching, worship, and connection opportunities available online, Christians (at least in North America) have a smorgasbord of possibilities for how they choose to "do church." For many of us, that means we're tempted to seek out people who are just like us, who like the same type of music we like, who preach about the topics we like to hear about, and who do it all in the kind of building we feel most comfortable in.

Paul warned against this very thing in his first letter to the church in Corinth, then described how the body should work together instead.

Read 1 Corinthians 12:12–27. Think about the body of believers you currently worship with on a regular basis. Is it a diverse group, reflecting the full body of Christ? Or is it more like a body with a whole bunch of eyes but no hands?

In week 3 of this study we read about the early church in Acts 2:42–47. Return to that passage now and read it again in the Christian Standard Bible translation, this time paying close attention to verses 44–46. How many times do you see the words "all" and "together"? What does that tell you about God's design for His church?

It's not practical or possible for every single believer on earth to worship in one place at one time. But God does value our unity, our ability to care for one another in community, and our dedication to worshiping Him as one body. As one we glorify Him, but worshiping together also increases our individual joy in knowing that we aren't alone in loving the Lord.

> God values our unity, our ability to care for one another in community, and our dedication to worshiping Him as one body.

Read Hebrews 10:24–25. What does this passage tell you about the importance of celebrating God together? How does that affect your view of the church?

The Psalms are full of invitations to rejoice in the Lord, invitations that call us to worship together as one. Psalm 95:1–2 says, "Come, let us sing to the LORD! Let us shout joyfully to the Rock of our salvation. Let us come to him with thanksgiving. Let us sing psalms of praise to him." Psalm 100:1 says, "Let the whole earth shout triumphantly to the LORD!" (CSB). And the book of Psalms closes with the words, "Let everything that breathes praise the LORD. Hallelujah!" (150:6 CSB).

Let us sing . . .

Let us shout . . .

Let the whole earth shout . . .

Let everything that breathes praise the Lord . . .

It's clear that God desires us to rejoice together. Whenever we get the opportunity to do that, we must approach Him with reverence and awe (Heb. 12:28) and with thankful hearts (Col. 3:16). That posture doesn't leave room for grumbling about the ways a worship service might not meet our expectations—but it does help us grow in love, obedience, and joy.

Take time to reread Psalm 100:1–2, as well as Hebrews 12:28–29 and Colossians 3:15–17. Put together, these instructions for worship—make a joyful noise, approach with reverence and awe, be thankful—make up a holy recipe for finding joy in community. What parts of the body are absent from the community you join for worship? How could you invite in others who might be the missing "ingredients" in your community?

_____

_____

_____

Learning the customs and traditions of other believers can bring us great joy and lead us into deeper relationships with one another and with God—but it can be hard! How can you courageously seek the joy God has for you in worship with others?

_____

_____

_____

_____

Reflect on this prayer and make it your own today:

Heavenly Father, thank You for creating Your children so perfectly unique. But thank You for also creating us to perfectly fit together as one body! Forgive me, Lord, for wanting to have it my way rather than finding joy in the harmony of our different voices. Please give me the courage to build bridges and join hands with believers, no matter what kind of joyful noise we make. Amen.

Praise him with the tambourine and dancing;
    praise him with strings and flutes!
Praise him with a clash of cymbals;
    praise him with loud clanging cymbals.
Let everything that breathes sing praises to the LORD!
Praise the LORD!

Psalm 150:4–6

While attending a women's conference a few years ago, I participated in packing food for people in Guatemala. In one hour, about fifty women packed 10,600 meals. As we stood around tables in our bright orange hairnets, dipping large serving spoons into nutritious dehydrated meals and packaging them, we chatted, laughed, and listened to music.

Soon one of the women in my group began nodding in time with the music's beat and singing along. Her actions were contagious, and before long our entire group—women from their twenties to their eighties—began nodding along. Then our shoulders began to shimmy and our hips began to sway. We were rocking out! Even the quietest in the bunch tapped their feet and gave it some rhythm.

Our group was made up of women from all walks of life—different ages, different backgrounds, and certainly different musical preferences. If you'd taken a poll and asked our favorite song or artist, you probably would have gotten fifty different answers. And yet, in that moment, the specific genre of music didn't matter. The notes and even the words weren't the point. What mattered was our shared joy in being the hands and feet of Jesus—and doing it together.

Together, as one, we were feeding the hungry, serving "the least of these" (Matt. 25:40)—and we were having a blast doing it! Our joy didn't come from the music or letting go for a bit to dance while we worked. No, we were celebrating the fact that we had the privilege of being Christ's hands to those less fortunate than we are.

Seeing God use a group of women, who just hours before had been strangers, to provide for our brothers and sisters in a completely different country was awesome. Better understanding how He loves us deeply and personally was enough to bring us to our knees—and to a dance party.

For every thousand meals packed, a bell rang out and we shouted and cheered and danced with all our might—and then laughed over the pure joy we felt. It was deliriously wonderful—and worshipful.

—GINGER KOLBABA

Think about a time when you've worked together with a group to serve others. How did that experience point you to God? Describe that here.

_____

_____

_____

_____

_____

Something special happens when we join with other believers to serve, to worship, to do anything that honors God. As we discussed earlier this week, joy that's shared multiplies, growing deeper and wider for each person involved. Likewise, the happiness that we feel when we lean into God-honoring work grows exponentially when we do that work in community.

We see this in the book of Acts, as the church is founded and then carries the gospel into the world. Paul and Barnabas were two of the early church leaders who were called to travel and share the good news of Jesus, and they found great joy in doing so. Later Paul wrote to the believers in Philippi of his hope that they would also experience this kind of shared joy: "Is there any encouragement from belonging to Christ? Any comfort from his love? Any fellowship together in the Spirit? Are your hearts tender and compassionate? Then make me truly happy by agreeing wholeheartedly with each other, loving one another, and working together with one mind and purpose" (Phil. 2:1–2).

If we're being honest, sometimes it's an inconvenience to join forces with others in a project or cause. It often feels easier to just do things ourselves rather than taking time to recruit others to help. After all, we'd have to slow down long enough to explain things and then— hardest of all!—compromise about how the work gets done. But when we refuse to collaborate, we rob ourselves of the joy of being part of Christ's body. And we might just lose an opportunity to show the world an example of God's love.

Think of a time when you worked with other Christians to accomplish a goal. What did you want to accomplish together? Knowing that the main goal of the collective body of Christ is to spread the gospel, how does that affect how you see and treat your sisters and brothers in Christ?

Paul wasn't the only one urging believers to work together and serve one another. Read 1 Peter 4:8–10. What gifts have you used in working with and serving others? How might you do that again in the future? What holds you back from serving?

Part of the joy found in working together is simply the delight of being able to show kindness and care for others. In Ginger's story, she and the other women were overjoyed to help feed the hungry. Their gratitude for the opportunity to do something good for someone else, combined with the satisfaction of doing so alongside other women, overflowed in a dancing and singing type of joy.

Once again, Paul expresses some of these same feelings of gratitude for the chance to do the Lord's work: "I thank Christ Jesus our Lord, who has given me strength to do his work. He considered me trustworthy and appointed me to serve him" (1 Tim. 1:12).

If we read that passage in context (1:12–17), we see that Paul was overwhelmed by God's mercy and goodness in allowing a great sinner like himself to participate in the work of sharing the gospel. Facing that truth, Paul couldn't help but celebrate and praise God. In the same way, when we realize how astonishing it is that the God of the universe is inviting us into His work, our joy compels us to share the gospel with others.

Read Psalm 8, then take a few minutes to consider the enormous gift God offers us through opportunities to work with Him. How does this change your understanding of service and good deeds? How do you feel led to respond—to God and to others around you?

_____

_____

_____

_____

_____

We don't have to pack thousands of meals for people in another country to find joy in serving God with others. It can be as simple as drawing pictures with your kids for senior citizens in a retirement home, or inviting a friend to join you in delivering canned goods to a food bank or sewing blankets for a local hospital. You can join groups already serving in some way—a group from your church, your kids' school, or perhaps a service organization in your community. The opportunities for serving the Lord are as numerous as our reasons to rejoice in Him!

> **The opportunities for serving the Lord are as numerous as our reasons to rejoice in Him!**

Read Philippians 2:1–2 again. Rewrite the passage in your own words, describing the blessings you've received from God and how you will show Him your thanks.

_____

_____

_____

_____

_____

_____

It can feel a little scary to invite others into a work you're passionate about, and it can be just as scary to openly celebrate and praise God for what He's doing through you. Read about Miriam (Exod. 15:19–21) and David (2 Sam. 6:14–15). How will you use their examples and what you've learned in this study to pursue joy by serving and worshiping God in community with others?

_____

_____

_____

_____

Reflect on this prayer and make it your own today:

Dear God, thank You! Thank You for inviting me into the holy work You're doing here on earth. I know I'm only worthy because of what Jesus has done for me, and I am so grateful. And I don't want to keep this good news and this joy to myself, Lord! Please give me the courage to reach out to others, joining them in serving You and celebrating Your goodness. Amen.

Rejoice with those who rejoice; weep with those who weep. Live in harmony with one another.

Romans 12:15–16 CSB

I stared at the tiny bundle of the baby in my friend's arms. He was less than a week old, smaller than he had looked in the photos she sent me. I watched him sleep, the way his pursed lips exhaled a small stream of air. He was perfect, of course. Week-old babies always are.

I felt so much at that moment—emotions so vast and varied—I could hardly articulate what was happening within me. My friend was a mom now. It was new and exciting and wonderful! She was fierce and incredible and had brought a beautiful tiny human into our world.

But I couldn't shake the pain that pricked inside me. *What if all of this—a new baby, a good marriage, a lovely home—doesn't happen for me? What if my life doesn't end up looking how I want it to?*

I blinked back tears and smiled at my beautiful friend. She was telling me her birth story. I wanted to hear all of it, and pride swelled up within me as I listened to what she had done.

The pain in my heart was real, though. The loneliness of being single can creep in unexpectedly and wrench at my heart. Most days I feel content and grateful, like I'm right where God wants me, but there are moments when it's as though a floodlight suddenly flicks on to show me all I am missing.

Later, I was honest with another friend about how hard it was for me. I didn't want to ignore what my feelings were telling me. But in that moment, when my friend shared her newborn son and her fears and joys over this new season of motherhood, I pushed down the pain and chose to rejoice with her.

I held her tiny son in my arms, stroking his soft, downy hair. With her little boy staring up at me, I knew we had much to rejoice about.

—ALIZA LATTA

Have you ever struggled to celebrate someone's good news because of the pain it caused you? How did you handle those competing emotions?

One of the most fascinating—and sometimes frustrating—things about human emotion is our capacity for feeling more than one thing at a time. Fortunately, as we discussed in week 3, God knows us better than anyone because He created us. The Bible is full of practical instruction about how to love God well and how to love others well within the reality of our emotional human condition.

Remember, when asked what are the greatest commandments, Jesus didn't hesitate: love God and love others. Everything else depends on these two commandments (Matt. 22:37–40). And though they are simple, Jesus knew they wouldn't be easy for us to follow. That's why, on the night before His crucifixion, He reassured the disciples that they wouldn't be left alone to live out everything He'd taught them. The Father would send the Spirit.

The Holy Spirit is given many different titles in Scripture. Depending on which English translation of John's Gospel you read, He's called the Helper (ESV), the Advocate (NIV), the Comforter (KJV), and the Counselor (CSB). Each of these names, however, points to Jesus's promise that the Holy Spirit will teach and remind believers about the things He taught.

Read John 14:18–26. Imagine you were one of Jesus's disciples. How do you think you would have felt hearing His words that day?

As you reflect on the passage above, ask the Holy Spirit to bring to mind ways He has counseled, comforted, or helped you. For example, has He ever brought Scripture to your mind exactly when you needed it? Record what you hear from Him.

As the early church grew, the apostle Paul planted and nurtured many new churches, sharing the good news and teachings of Jesus with new believers. His letters are full of detailed directions for how to live as Christ followers. Paul knew that learning how to love God and love others was crucial for believers everywhere as they grew in their faith and lived out their witness to the life-changing love of Jesus.

In the book of Romans, Paul instructs the believers to love one another so sincerely and so deeply that it seems as if they're trying to "outdo one another" (Rom. 12:10 ESV). Then he tells them, "Rejoice with those who rejoice, weep with those who weep" (12:15 ESV). At first glance this is an easy one to check off our "how to be a good Christian" list. But when we dig a little deeper—and when we're honest with ourselves—we know that this can be a really hard thing to do.

While it might seem like the weeping part would be more difficult, most of us have enough empathy to feel sadness, disappointment, grief, or regret when our friends are hurting. But the rejoicing part? Now *that* can feel like a much taller order!

When you've been trying to conceive for months or even years and your friend announces her third pregnancy . . .

When your sister tells you about her latest promotion at work on the same day you lost a big client . . .

When you're invited to another wedding while wondering if you'll ever meet someone to spend your life with . . .

When you open the invitation to a house-warming party as you look around your cramped apartment . . .

Celebrating with those who are receiving the blessings you long for can be gut-wrenching. At times it seems impossible. And yet, more than once in Scripture, we're told to rejoice with one another. We're told to put one another's needs above our own (Phil. 2:4), to put aside any jealousy, anger, or bitterness we might feel (Eph. 4:31–32). We're told to rejoice with our brothers and sisters in Christ (1 Cor. 12:26).

What do you do when your feelings seem to totally contradict what
Scripture tells us to do? Take a moment to read Matthew 19:23–26
and Philippians 4:10–13. What do these examples tell us about
seemingly impossible tasks?

_____

_____

_____

_____

_____

The inner turmoil we feel when we struggle to rejoice with those
who rejoice is no surprise to God. He knows we live in a broken world,
and He knows we have unfulfilled longings. He knows that most of us
are capable of experiencing more than one emotion at a time and that
we might find it difficult to reach for joy while wading through darker feelings.

God knows we can't live out His instructions in
our own ability or strength. That's why He gives us
the Holy Spirit. In addition to guiding and training
us in all the ways of Christ, the Spirit can also teach
us how to choose joy for others, even as our own
heart breaks. He can comfort us in our own pain
and counsel us in how to rejoice anyway. And we can find joy in knowing our heavenly Father loves us so much that He gives us exactly what
we need to experience genuine empathy, compassion, and happiness
for those around us.

> God knows we can't live out His instructions in our own ability or strength. That's why He gives us the Holy Spirit.

Read the prayer in Lamentations 3:18–26. Rewrite this prayer in your own words. Let it be a reminder that even when you feel pain and sorrow, you can still rejoice in the Lord and for others.

How does today's study challenge you? In what area of your life do you need courage and counsel from the Holy Spirit to live differently this week?

Reflect on this prayer and make it your own today:

God, thank You for knowing how much help I need to follow You and live according to Your will and Your Word! Thank You for the Holy Spirit and for every word of Scripture. Please forgive me for the times I've let bitterness or envy get in the way of rejoicing with others. When I'm tempted to let my feelings trump my obedience to You, help me remember the joy of my salvation. I love You and I want to love others as You do. Amen.

notes

Week 1 What Is Joy?

1. "Brené Brown on Joy and Gratitude," YouTube video, November 28, 2012, https://youtube.com/watch?v=2IjSHUc7TXM.

2. John Piper, "How Do You Define Joy?," Desiring God, July 25, 2015, https://www.desiringgod.org/articles/how-do-you-define-joy.

3. Henri J. M. Nouwen, *You Are the Beloved: Daily Meditations for Spiritual Living* (New York: Convergent Books, 2017), 169.

4. Nouwen, *You Are the Beloved*, 380.

5. Chrystal Hurst, "Find the Joy," *Chrystal Evans Hurst* (blog), December 9, 2019, https://chrystalevanshurst.com/find-the-joy/.

6. "Mother Teresa on Prayer," *Franciscan Spirit* (blog), April 22, 2017, https://www.franciscanmedia.org/franciscan-spirit-blog/mother-teresa-on-prayer.

7. "For the Joy Set Before Him," sermon preached December 26, 2010, Southside Church of Christ, Fort Myers, FL, https://southsidechurchofchrist.com/sermons/for-the-joy-set-before-him.html.

8. C. S. Lewis, *The Four Loves* (1960; repr. New York: Harcourt Brace, 1991), 121.

9. "Dr. Brené Brown on Joy: It's Terrifying," SuperSoul Sunday, March 17, 2013, Oprah Winfrey Network, https://www.youtube.com/watch?v=RKV0BWSPfOw.

Week 2 Joy in the Lord

1. Oswald Chambers, "My Joy . . . Your Joy," *My Utmost for His Highest*, August 31, https://utmost.org/classic/my-joy-your-joy-classic/.

2. Dolly Parton, @DollyParton, Twitter, September 12, 2013, https://twitter.com/DollyParton/status/378249735791853568.

Week 3 Joy in Who God Made You to Be

1. A. W. Tozer, *Who Put Jesus on the Cross? And Other Questions of the Christian Faith* (Camp Hill, PA: WingSpread Publishers, 2009), 154.

Week 5 Joy in the Bad Times

1. Elisabeth Kübler-Ross, *On Death and Dying* (London: Routledge, 2005).

2. Sara Frankl and Mary Carver, *Choose Joy: Finding Hope and Purpose When Life Hurts* (New York: FaithWords, 2017), 27.

about the authors

Mary Carver is a writer and speaker who lives for good books, spicy queso, and television marathons—but lives because of God's grace. She writes about giving up on perfect and finding truth in unexpected places at MaryCarver.com and on Instagram @marycarver. Mary and her husband live in Kansas City with their two daughters.

Karina Allen is devoted to helping women live out their unique calling and building authentic community through practical application of Scripture in an approachable, winsome manner. Connect with her on Instagram @karina268.

Lucretia Berry, PhD, is the creator of Brownicity.com. She is a wife, a mom of three, and a former college professor whose passion for racial healing led her to author *What LIES Between Us: Fostering First Steps toward Racial Healing* and to speak at TEDx Charlotte and Q Ideas Charlotte. Find her at brownicity.com and on Instagram @lucretiaberry.

Kaitlyn Bouchillon is a writer who is learning to see God's goodness in the beautiful ordinary of right now. She is the author of *Even If Not: Living, Loving, and Learning in the in Between,* and she'll never turn down an iced latte. Find her at kaitlynbouchillon.com and on Instagram @kaitlyn_bouch.

Stephanie Bryant is the cofounder of (in)courage and hosts the *Jesus Led Adventure* podcast. She enjoys spending her days with her husband and their miracle daughter on their farm. Find Stephanie on Instagram @stephaniesbryant and at stephaniebryant.me.

Grace P. Cho is the (in)courage editorial manager. In the middle of her years in church ministry, she sensed God moving her toward writing, to use her words to lead. She coaches writers, mentors leaders, and believes that telling our stories can change the world. Connect with her on Instagram @gracepcho.

Robin Dance is the author of *For All Who Wander*, is married to her college sweetheart, and is as Southern as sugar-shocked tea. An empty nester with a full life, she's determined to age with grace and laugh at the days to come. Connect with her at robindance.me and on Instagram @robindance.me.

Dorina Lazo Gilmore-Young is a blogger, a speaker, and the author of *Glory Chasers* and *Flourishing Together*. She specializes in helping people navigate grief and flourish in community. An award-winning children's author, Dorina has also served as a journalist, missionary, and social entrepreneur. She and her husband are raising three brave girls. Find her at dorinagilmore.com and on Instagram @dorinagilmore.

Becky Keife is the community manager for (in)courage. She shares funny stories and biblical truths as a speaker and is the author of *No Better Mom for the Job*. Becky loves hiking shady SoCal trails with her husband and three spirited sons. Connect with her on Instagram @beckykeife and at beckykeife.com.

Ginger Kolbaba is a bestselling, award-winning author, editor, and speaker. She has written or contributed to more than thirty-five books, including *Breakthrough*, recently released as a major motion picture. She is a sassy contemplative and a fun-loving traveler who loves Jesus most of all. Visit her at gingerkolbaba.com.

Aliza Latta is a Canadian writer, journalist, and artist who is a huge fan of telling stories. She writes about faith and young adulthood at alizalatta.com, and is the author of the novel *Come Find Me, Sage Parker*. Find her on Instagram @alizalatta.

Anna Rendell is the (in)courage digital content manager and lives in Minnesota with her husband and their kids. She loves a good book and a great latte. Anna is the author of *Pumpkin Spice for Your Soul* and *A Moment of Christmas*. Visit her at AnnaRendell.com and on Instagram @annaerendell.

Michelle Reyes, PhD, is an Indian American pastor's wife, writer, and activist. She is vice president of the Asian American Christian Collaborative and writes regularly on faith, culture, and justice. Michelle lives in Austin, Texas, with her husband and two kids. Follow her on Instagram @michelleamireyes.

Kristen Strong, author of *Back Roads to Belonging*, is a belonging helper, change mentor, and welcoming friend. She and her US Air Force veteran husband, David, have three children and live in Colorado Springs. Find her at kristenstrong.com and on Instagram @kristenstrong.

Jennifer Ueckert is a mixed-media artist living in rural Nebraska. She is married to her patient and supportive husband. Jennifer wants her artwork to reflect the beauty of God. You can read her words and see more of her art at studiojru.com and on Instagram @studioJRU.

Bible Studies to Refresh Your Soul

In these six-week Bible studies, your friends at (in)courage will help you dive deep into real-life issues, the transforming power of God's Word, and what it means to courageously live your faith.

100 Days of Hope and Peace

In this 100-day devotional, the (in)courage community reaches into the grief and pain of both crisis and ordinary life. Each day includes a key Scripture, a heartening devotion, and a prayer to remind you that God is near and hope is possible. You won't find tidy bows or trite quick fixes, just arrows pointing you straight to Jesus.

(in)courage welcomes you

to a place where authentic, brave women connect deeply with God and others. Through the power of shared stories and meaningful resources, (in)courage champions women and celebrates the strength Jesus gives to live out our calling as God's daughters. Together we build community, celebrate diversity, and **become women of courage**.

Join us at **www.incourage.me**
& connect with us on social media!